Actionable Performance Measurement

Also Available from ASQ Quality Press:

Measurement Matters: How Effective Assessment Drives Business and Safety Performance
Brooks Carder and Patrick Ragan

Performance Measurement Explained: Designing and Implementing Your State-of-the-Art System
Bjørn Andersen and Tom Fagerhaug

The Path to Profitable Measures: 10 Steps to Feedback That Fuels Performance
Mark W. Morgan

The Process-Focused Organization: A Transition Strategy for Success
Robert A. Gardner

Healthcare Performance Measurement: Systems Design and Evaluation
Vahé A. Kazandjian and Terry R. Lied

Linking Customer and Employee Satisfaction to the Bottom Line
Derek Allen and Morris Wilburn

Process Quality Control: Troubleshooting and Interpretation of Data, Fourth Edition
Ellis R. Ott, Edward G. Schilling, and Dean V. Neubauer

Managing with Conscience for Competitive Advantage
Pete Geissler

To request a complimentary catalog of ASQ Quality Press publications, call 800-248-1946, or visit our website at http://qualitypress.asq.org.

Actionable Performance Measurement

A Key to Success

Marvin T. Howell, P.E.

ASQ Quality Press
Milwaukee, Wisconsin

American Society for Quality, Quality Press, Milwaukee 53203
© 2006 by Marvin T. Howell
All rights reserved. Published 2005
Printed in the United States of America

12 11 10 09 08 07 06 05   5 4 3 2 1

Library of Congress Cataloging-in-Publication Data

Howell, Marvin T., 1936–
    Actionable performance measurement: a key to success / Marvin T. Howell.
      p. cm.
    Includes bibliographical references and index.
    ISBN 0-87389-664-5 (pbk. : alk. paper)
    1. Organizational effectiveness—Measurement. 2. Performance—Measurement. 3. Total
quality management. 4. Performance standards. I. Title.

    HD58.9.H69 2006
    658.4′013–dc22

                      2005020443

ISBN-13: 978-0-87389-664-1
ISBN-10: 0-87389-664-5

Publisher: William A. Tony
Acquisitions Editor: Annemieke Hytinen
Project Editor: Paul O'Mara
Production Administrator: Randall Benson

ASQ Mission: The American Society for Quality advances individual, organizational, and
community excellence worldwide through learning, quality improvement, and knowledge
exchange.

Attention Bookstores, Wholesalers, Schools, and Corporations: ASQ Quality Press books,
videotapes, audiotapes, and software are available at quantity discounts with bulk
purchases for business, educational, or instructional use. For information, please contact
ASQ Quality Press at 800-248-1946, or write to ASQ Quality Press, P.O. Box 3005,
Milwaukee, WI 53201-3005.

To place orders or to request a free copy of the ASQ Quality Press Publications Catalog,
including ASQ membership information, call 800-248-1946. Visit our website at
www.asq.org or http://qualitypress.asq.org.

♾ Printed on acid-free paper

Quality Press
600 N. Plankinton Avenue
Milwaukee, Wisconsin 53203
Call toll free 800-248-1946
Fax 414-272-1734
www.asq.org
http://qualitypress.asq.org
http://standardsgroup.asq.org
E-mail: authors@asq.org

AMERICAN SOCIETY
FOR QUALITY™

To my wife Jackie, Administrative Assistant Nancy Sharp,
Air Force Civil Engineering, Florida Power and Light
Company, JUSE Counselors, and my past Quality Clients.

Contents

CD-ROM Contents

The following files* are available on the accompanying CD-ROM for this book. To access them, you will need Adobe Acrobat and word processing software such as Microsoft Word.

Appendix A Modified Nominal Group Technique

> file name: ModifiedNGT.pdf

Appendix B Brainstorming

> file name: Brainstorming.pdf

Appendix C Assessment of an Existing Measurement System

> file name: Assessment.pdf

Appendix D Metrics Awareness Questionnaire

> file name: MetricAwarenessQ.pdf

Appendix E A Message to Leaders

> file name: LeadersQ.pdf

Actionable Performance Measurement: A Key to Success—Student Workbook

> file name: StudentWorkbook.doc

Figures and Tables

Acronyms

AIM—analyze, improve, manage (monitor, control, and improve)
APQC—American Productivity and Quality Center
BOATS—business objectives attainment tracking system
BOATS-P and BOATS-R—business objectives attainment tracking system. P = process, R = results
CAPDO—check act plan do
COPIS—customer output process input supplier
COPQ—cost of poor quality
CSF—critical success factors
CSI—customer satisfaction index
DPM—defects per million
DMAIIC—define measure analyze improvement implement control
ESI—employee satisfaction index
FedEx—Federal Express Company
FPL—Florida Power and Light Company
FMEA—failure modes effects analysis
5 Ws and 1 H—who, why, what, when, and where plus how
GPRA—Government Performance Requirement Act
JUSE—Union of Japanese Scientists and Engineers
PIs—performance indicators
POEM—problem or purpose observe evaluate measure
QC—quality control
ISO—International Standards Organization
KRAs—key result areas
MBNQA—Malcolm Baldrige National Quality Award
NGT—nominal group technique
PDCA—plan do check act—the Deming wheel
PDSA—plan do study act—the Shewhart cycle
RATER—responsiveness assurance tangible empathy reliability
SIPOC—supplier inputs process outputs customers
SIPOOC—supplier inputs process outputs outcomes customers
SMART—specific measurable actionable reviewed time-framed
SU—service unavailability
SAIDI—service availability interruption duration index
SQIs—statistical quality indicators used by FedEx
VPs—vice presidents

Preface

Throughout an Air Force career, with Florida Power and Light Company, and then as president and director of Quality Management Technologies Inc., the author observed the tremendous importance of actionable performance indicators (metrics). Any improvement effort really starts with a good metric. You may have a problem that drives improvement, but if you don't have a good measure, you may improve the operation, process, or job without being able to verify that you did.

The author has observed many organizations that have a "flood of indicators." They feel they must be able to explain everything, so they measure just about everything that occurs. Performance indicators or metrics cost money to maintain. When you have too many corporate measures (more than 30), some important ones may get lost and no action taken when the trends go in the wrong direction. The right thing to do is to have just enough measures to drive corporate performance and manage your key and supporting processes. The measures must be actionable—that's the main characteristic of a performance indicator or metric. In other words, they must drive action when necessary and show the results of the actions.

Key result areas (KRAs), tied to mission and customers' requirements, are essential for strategic planning and continuous improvement. This book provides a simple process to do this. The KRAs are the areas any organization needs to improve to get maximum benefits. Examples are quality, cost, schedule, safety, management, delivery, timeliness, and security. They are high level, and measures need to be developed for each one. Then for departments, business units, the key processes, and key jobs, the KRAs and the measures supporting them at all levels provide the linkage that enables efficient and effective measurement and improvement.

Other performance measurement efforts such as balanced score cards (Kaplan, 1992) have been useful but more difficult to link than KRAs. KRAs simply tell what the customers will receive when organization(s) or companies perform their core mission.

Most books on performance measurement cover some elements, but hardly any give you complete coverage. It is the author's intent to accomplish this and provide a book with valuable information to be used by:

- Any professional/executive, manager, engineer, supervisor, or facilitator charged with making improvements at the corporate, department, business unit, process, or job level or a team accomplishing a specific mission.

- Six Sigma practitioners who need good performance indicators that influence or measure the key processes of the organization.

- Consultants hired to help any organization improve its performance. Also, internal consultants with a mission to improve organizational performance.

- Upper management and corporate staff deciding on breakthrough improvements, reengineering the organization, or executing an excellent strategic plan. They can be from industrial production companies, service industries, large hospitals, educational institutions, or most midsize and large business enterprises.

- Quality coordinators, facilitators, and practitioners can use this book in developing corporate measures, process indicators, department measures, and key jobs, as well as measuring teams'successes.

The author has found that many people (consultants, managers, Six Sigma and quality practitioners) talk a good language about metrics or performance indicators. However, when someone asks them to help develop a good measure or evaluate one's effectiveness, they don't have a process for doing so. This book gives them that process.

Even the Union of Japanese Scientists and Engineers (JUSE) counselors, who are world-famous teachers on problem solving, seven quality control tools, and other important areas, did not provide a method or process in developing good metrics during their counseling sessions with FPL during its successful pursuit of the Deming Prize. This book not only gives a proven process, but also 11 methods for developing new performance indicators and the knowledge and tools for evaluating existing indicators.

Throughout the book, each chapter has learning objectives and a glossary. The readers are encouraged to read material and then go back to ask, "Did I understand the learning objectives, and did I learn sufficiently to meet them?"

Chapter 1 provides an introduction to metrics. It defines metrics, importance of measurement, and characteristics of a good measurement. It covers how measures can be manipulated and steps that can be taken to minimize or eliminate this from happening. Some organizations' measurement efforts have failed. The causes are outlined so you can prevent this from happening in your organization.

Chapter 2 is about management by metrics. This chapter shows what an organization dedicated to performance measurement looks like. The strategic planning process and key products along the way are presented. An original concept of keeping track of strategic objectives' implementation from an activity and results viewpoint is presented respectively as BOATS-P (business objectives attainment tracking system–process) and BOATS-R (business objectives attainment tracking system–results). A comprehensive organizational planning model shows where measurement is needed to ensure organizational success. Small business needs and uses are also mentioned.

Chapter 3 is about the metrics development process. The process is outlined, and the first four steps of the seven-step process are covered in detail: Step 1, identify purpose and establish objectives; Step 2, determine whether existing traditional indicators are available and are appropriate; Step 3, generate new possible performance indicators; and Step 4, evaluate indicators for effectiveness.

In Step 1, a technique to help define the problem is shown. Step 2 is about traditional indicators, of which all industries have some. These are useful in that they facilitate benchmarking, because normally the data are captured under the same rules. Step 3, generating new possible performance indicators, is the meat of this chapter and the heart of the book. Most authors mention this but don't provide methods to assist in identifying new performance indicators. The author shows 11 methods that can be very helpful to an individual or team responsible for developing an actionable performance measure or measurement system. Appendices A and B outline Using Brainstorming and Nominal Group Technique in developing new measures. Criteria that describe what a good performance indicator contains or meets are presented.

In Chapter 4, on constructing the indicator graph and the metrics package, a step-by-step procedure is provided. Line graphs and bar graphs (plus combinations) are the most used graphs. The United States Air Force metrics package—consisting of operational definition (defines what will be included, who gathers data and when), measurement (chart selection, baseline data from six months to a year of past data), presentation format (formula, graph, responsible person, data collection information)—is provided to give a framework for performing this step.

Chapter 5 provides eight methods of setting targets. The author believes this is the most comprehensive and clear presentation on this subject. It is Step 6 of our metrics development process. Without a target, there is no incentive to improve. Too tight a target can lower morale and motivation. Setting a realistic but stretch target is the goal.

Two case studies show how teams typically plan and execute a search for performance measures. One team ends up in failure, although the members thought they had done an excellent job. The second effort is successful. Their tasks are different, but by following the process they were able to achieve their mission in an exemplary manner. Measurement teams can learn from both cases.

Organizations have a lot of indicators, some even a flood of indicators. Criteria are set forth to assist in the decision of whether you should keep or get rid of an existing indicator.

The seven-step "monitor and take action" is shown in Chapter 6. The seven quality improvement tools are discussed, and how to construct and use them is outlined. A seven-step problem-solving technique linked to the plan-do-check-act Deming Wheel is outlined. A simple, demonstrative example clearly shows how the seven-step process flows and how the tools apply and contribute to the steps.

Now that the process has been explained and examples provided to show how to apply the process, some uses of the measures can be explored. In Chapter 7, measuring and jump-starting processes and using performance measures to benchmark to improve organization's key processes performance are demonstrated. e-Bay process examples are used to show how the use of a performance measure can immediately improve performance and outcomes.

Sometimes organizations need to bring together a lot of metrics that have different units of measures (that is, pounds, inches, or numbers.) Thankfully, there is a way of measuring apples and oranges. It is called the objectives matrix. Chapter 8 shows step by step how to use this technique and rolls up indicators into one performance measure.

Chapter 9 focuses on the customers, internal and external. Questions such as "What are our customer's requirements?" "How well are we meeting these requirements?" "How can we capture the customer's voice and use it to improve how we do business?" are discussed, and techniques, tools, and concepts are explored. The development of a customer survey (internal and external) is covered to give the readers ideas and process in developing their surveys. The analysis of surveys is discussed. A customer satisfaction model is presented; gap analysis and developing a customer satisfaction index are fully developed. Customers are why we are in business; we must get new customers and retain our present ones. These tools, techniques, and concepts can help any organization in achieving this paramount goal. An MBNQA Survey, "Are We Making Progress as Leaders?," is shown in Appendix E. Administering this survey to leadership, recapping the results, analyzing the data, developing conclusions and recommendations will help you understand the process better as well as improve your organization's performance capabilities.

Along with the customers, owners, or leaders of the company or organization, employees are a major stakeholder. Employee focus, satisfaction, and measurement are covered in Chapter 10. Employee focus groups and surveys, along with some other measurement tools, are discussed.

Now that the reader understands how to develop and use performance indicators, the next challenge is participating on a corporate, department, or business unit measurement team commissioned to develop a new performance measurement system. The process for accomplishing this important and difficult test is covered in Chapter 11. Appendix C gives a survey that can assist in evaluating the present existing measurement system. Appendix D provides a method of assessing present metrics awareness. These results are essential in the modification of a present system or developing a new one. Chapter 12 provides a conclusion that restates some of the major elements included in the book. If any of them are not clear, the reader is encouraged to go back to the area and review.

Appendices A and B show how to use nominal group technique and brainstorming, respectively, to generate new ideas. Appendix C is an assessment for an existing measurement system, and the questionnaire in Appendix D measures metric awareness. Appendix E is the Malcolm Baldrige National Quality Award "Are We Making Progress as Leaders?" questionnaire.

On the accompanying CD-ROM are the five appendices as well as a complete student workbook, which enables any organization or consultant to teach a three-day intensive seminar that provides key personnel with the performance measurement knowledge covered in this book. Included is the material to be presented, questions and answers, and exercises. The length of time required for each activity is stated. The author has presented this material in numerous seminars.

1

Introduction to Metrics

A good metric will tell you how things are going. If the indicator is showing better performance, then the performance actually is better and vice versa.

1.1 OBJECTIVES

1. Understand an indicator and the types.

2. Be familiar that indicators can vary by organization level and particular needs.

3. Understand indicators can be manipulated and what you can do to prevent or minimize.

4. Know the primary reasons indicators fail (not used properly).

1.2 GLOSSARY

actionable—If trend is going the wrong way on an indicator, it drives the correct action to be taken to improve performance. Actions are developed through evaluation and analysis and are solutions or countermeasures.

effectiveness—How well the plan or goal was achieved.

efficiency—How well resources are used compared to the plan.

indicator—A graph with a target plotted over time to show progress. Has a unit of measure, title, data collection identified, and formula (if necessary).

manipulation—Makes the results of an indicator look good through some undesired action (cheating) such as falsifying data or changing data.

metric—An indicator that drives meaningful action.

performance indicators—Measures performance of an organization, processes, and/or jobs.

1.3 A METRIC

A metric is a measurement, taken over time, that communicates vital information about a process or activity. The major requirement for being a metric versus an indicator is that a metric must drive appropriate action. In other words, if you are off target, the metric shows you that and enables you to start action to get back on target. It is nothing more than a meaningful measure. Performance indicators and metrics are basically the same and often are used interchangeably. Indicators can be counts (such as number of widgets produced) and may not be either a metric or a performance indicator. Metrics are normally process measures. This book will address all indicators because outcome, supplier metrics measures, output measures, and others are also very important.

Performance indicators come from outputs or their outcomes.

Metrics or performance measures come from processes and their inputs, outputs, and outcomes (see Figure 1.1).

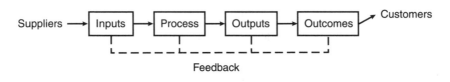

Figure 1.1 Process diagram.

Measures can come from any one of these plus a combination of two such as:

$$\text{Productivity} = \frac{\text{Output(s)}}{\text{Inputs}}$$

Inputs are supplier measures such as quality of materials received, timeliness of deliveries, cost of materials, tools, and equipment. Outputs are what the process produces: products, services, or information. Examples include the quantity of production or services, the defects or errors, and scrap produced. Outcome measures indicate whether customers are satisfied (customer satisfaction/retention), and they also look at results from the organization's viewpoint. Efficiency, throughput, yield, timeliness of delivery or service, cost versus budget, and reliability are a few examples important to an organization.

Figure 1.2 shows the relationship between an indicator, a metric, performance indicators, and control charts.

Normally, the author uses *performance indicator* and *metric* interchangeably because they both drive performance.

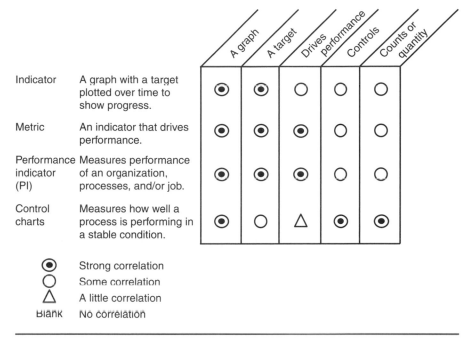

	A graph	A target	Drives performance	Controls	Counts or quantity
Indicator — A graph with a target plotted over time to show progress.	◉	◉	○	○	○
Metric — An indicator that drives performance.	◉	◉	◉	○	○
Performance indicator (PI) — Measures performance of an organization, processes, and/or job.	◉	◉	◉	○	○
Control charts — Measures how well a process is performing in a stable condition.	◉	○	△	◉	◉

◉ Strong correlation
○ Some correlation
△ A little correlation
Blank No correlation

Figure 1.2 Measures and their relationships.

All three (metrics, performance indicators, and control charts) are indicators.

Indicators can at times have different objectives—improvement or control. It has been the author's experience that most organizations have 80 percent of their indicators for control purposes or quantity counts and only 20 percent for improvement. If the management mind-set is for improvement using teams and encouraging teamwork, the controlling indicators can also become improvement indicators.

1.4 IMPORTANCE

Without metrics or performance indicators, you do not know how your process is performing, how well you are doing your job, and how well your organization is achieving its mission.

Metrics

- Provide early warning of problems or bottlenecks.

- Enable us to manage our processes, jobs, and organization.

- Provide basis for continuous improvement.

- Facilitate communications throughout the organization.

- Keep score on items of importance such as goals attainment.

1.5 CHARACTERISTICS OF GOOD METRICS

The characteristics or attributes of effective metrics are first simple and understandable. You do not want a formula that looks like a Ph.D. developed it. You want everyone to understand it and how they can help affect it positively. What is a good performance indicator? One that communicates to everyone involved the desired behavior. When performance improves, the indicator shows this improvement and vice versa.

The essence of continuous improvement is to keep turning the PDCA wheel or PDSA cycle. For each turn, some improvement results. PDCA (plan, do, check, act) represents how we think. Americans are great at the planning and doing phase, but instead of checking and taking action, we are ready to run to another planning and doing phase. To become world class, we must follow the entire wheel or cycle over and over again. This is how you achieve continual improvement. The PDSA is the same except C for check becomes S for study. PDSA was first mentioned in the early 1900s by Shewhart in a presentation. Dr. Deming, who was in attendance, took this concept to Japan, where "study" was changed to "check" because they felt it was closer to how people think (see Figure 1.3). The turn of the wheel occurs when you go all way around through the four phases. Then you start over and continue to improve in future efforts.

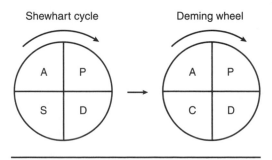

Figure 1.3 Shewhart cycle/Deming wheel.

If a stable process develops a problem, Dr. Noriaki Kano (counseling with Florida Power and Light in pursuit of the Deming Prize) says the situation calls for check, act, plan, do (CAPDO) (see Figure 1.4).

This is because the first thing you do is check. Without metrics, there would be no check or study. For continuous

Figure 1.4 CAPDO.

improvement efforts, understanding our processes, monitoring our measures, taking action when needed, and turning the PDCA wheel continuously are the keys to success.

A process is a sequence of activities that when accomplished produces a product or service. It has inputs (suppliers), the process itself, outputs and outcomes from customers receiving the products, profit margin (sales price − cost), and so forth.

The process described in Figure 1.5 is traditionally called SIPOO or IPOO or COPIS. It is simply described by how you emphasize the letters.

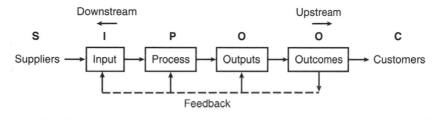

Figure 1.5 SIPOOC diagram.

Inputs are parts, suppliers, machines, equipment, and people to be used in the process. The process produces a product or service such as cars, plates, boxes or environmental cleanup, electricity, or transportation. Metrics may be necessary in all of the SIPOO areas. The eight metrics attributes are:

- Measurable

- Simple and understandable

- Meaningful; send the right message; drives appropriate action

- Timely, believable, and acceptable

- Well-defined and shows a trend

- Cost-effective

- Repeatable, auditable, and sensitive

- Customer-oriented

The most important attribute is that it is meaningful—it measures its purpose and drives the right action. The metric must have a good operational definition (an internal definition so everyone knows exactly what is included in the data). The metric must show a trend so that comparisons to standards—targets or control limits as appropriate—can be made. This is useful only if the data or information is timely so quick action can be taken if needed. Metrics must be cost effective. If the cost is excessive and one metric is of little importance, then naturally you would not collect the data. The metric must be auditable (if looked at by different people, the interpretation would be the same). It should be repeatable (the data are the same for same time periods). The attributes are simple and used to evaluate potential indicators by a knowledgeable group ranking them from 1 to 5 (5 being the best) and selecting the one with the highest score. This will be further explained in Chapter 3. The attributes can be made 10 by breaking out "believable" and "acceptable" into separate categories.

1.6 MALCOLM BALDRIGE NATIONAL QUALITY AWARD CRITERIA, DEMING PRIZE CRITERIA, AND ISO 9000 MANAGEMENT SYSTEM

The Malcolm Baldrige National Quality Award (MBNQA) was named after a secretary of commerce killed in a rodeo accident. Since 1987, this award has been presented by the U.S. Commerce Department to recognize American companies that excelled in quality improvement. Manufacturing companies, service companies, small businesses, and education and hospital (healthcare) organizations can receive awards annually if they meet the criteria well enough to be verified by the examiners. (For more information contact the American Society for Quality, www.asq.com.) The quality journey of the winners is shared on videos, quality conferences, benchmarking efforts, and so forth.

The Deming Prize has been awarded to individuals and organizations in Japan, and in 1989 the Florida Power and Light Company received the first overseas Deming Prize (followed by Phillips Taiwan in 1991 and AT&T Power Systems in 1994). The Union of Japanese Scientists and Engineers administers the Deming Prize. General criteria are available. To win the award, it is necessary to receive counseling from JUSE counselors such as Dr. Yoji Akao, Dr. Noriaki Kano, Dr. Yoshio Kondo, Dr. Hajime Makabe, and others. All are famous and extremely talented. A detailed and comprehensive review (audit) by JUSE counselors who have not participated in preparing the organization is conducted. Their findings are submitted to the JUSE executive committee, which decides whether an award is justified.

Pursuing either of these awards can help any company improve its quality and processes/performance. In addition, other companies' assessment reports and videos of winners can be useful information.

ISO 9000 is a series of international standards, 9001 is requirements, and 9004 is guidelines for performance improvement. ISO identifies basic requirements or standards for any organization's quality system, giving practical procedures and approaches that ensure that products and services meet customers' requirements. It is a useful basis upon which organizations can manage their business and achieve consistent quality products and/or consistent service. For more information, go to *www.iso.org*. ISO 14001 uses a PDCA approach to plan and implement an Environmental Management System (EMS). Goals, objectives, and measures are established to improve an organization's environmental performance.

1.7 TYPES OF INDICATORS

Organization
Process
Job/activities

Indicators can be described as strategic, business, tactical, organizational, process, supplier, or outcome. Each organization has at least three types of indicators: organizational, process, and job.

The organizational level is normally strategic or tactical. The process measures are of the key/critical processes, and the job consists of major functions, activities, and/or responsibilities for individuals to perform.

The title of the specific measure—efficiency, effectiveness, productivity, budget, quality, quality of workplace, innovation, customer satisfaction, utilization—can be used to describe it. You can be efficient and not effective or effective and not efficient. The objective is to be both efficient and effective. Efficient means good use of resources as planned where effectiveness means meeting your goals or objectives. An example of being inefficient but effective would be if a planner checks the job for installing a customer's electric meter; it is ready, so the job is scheduled, but the crew arrives to find that a truck had dumped gravel for the driveway where the ditch for the hookup was to go. The crew goes back two days later, installing the meter a day before the family moves into the house. That is effective but not efficient. Success is when we are both efficient and effective.

1.7.1 Efficiency Indicators

Efficiency indicators shows how well you used resources per the plan. Efficiency indicators (output/input) have both numerators and denominators. They can be of four categories. Productivity, which is output divided by input, is a special efficiency indicator.

Category	Indicators
1. Physical quantities Physical quantities (different than the numerator)	Square feet maintained Number of hourly maintenance people Number of orders per month Number of people processing orders Performance = $\dfrac{\text{Standard hours}}{\text{Actual hours worked}}$

(Continued)

(Continued)

Category	Indicators
2. Output in dollars Input in a physical quantity	Production cost Number of employees
	Production cost Total man hours
	Budget expended Total man hours used
3. Output in physical quantity Input price form	Number of units produced Production cost
	Number people trained Training cost
4. Output in dollars Input in dollars	Excess inventory dollars Total inventory dollars
	Total facilities improvement cost Total facilities plant value

Outputs

		Physical Quantity	Cost
Inputs	Physical Quantity	Category 1	Category 2
	Cost	Category 3	Category 4

Efficiency indicators can be of all four categories. Select the one that best measures your objective or build one using this philosophy or concept.

1.7.2 Effectiveness Indicators

Effectiveness indicators show how well the goals/targets were achieved. They are *outcome* measures. Examples are customer satisfaction, profit, customer retention, cost, schedule achievement, safety, and quality.

1.7.3 Balanced Scorecard/Sink's Seven

Sink (1989) describes seven measures as key to organizational performance. They are effectiveness, efficiency, quality, quality of work life (QWL), productivity, innovation, and budgetability/profitability. These seven measures are each important indicators. Kaplan used the balanced scorecard (1992, 1996) to measure finance, processes, learning and growth, and customers. The balanced scorecard also outlines a framework for translating a strategy into operational initiatives (see Figure 1.6).

Almost anything can be measured. Methods include an estimate, an assessment between 0 to 10, a survey with Likert scale (a scale that enables a participant to select degrees of performance or satisfaction; see Chapter 9), ranking, an index, or a finite measure where data are available.

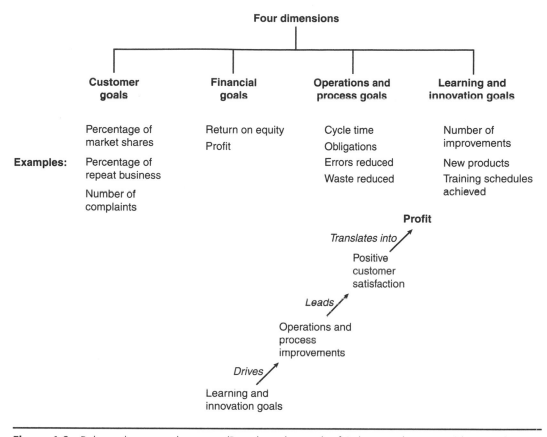

Figure 1.6 Balanced scorecard system. (Based on the work of Robert Kaplan & David Norton)

The finite measure is where we want to be in our measurement of corporate or process performance. If that is not possible, a lesser-desired measure should be selected.

1.7.4 Six Sigma Measurement Importance

Six Sigma concept has become very popular and has produced significant results in many companies. Six Sigma starts with the company's leaders. Their commitment, emphasis, support, and recognizing and communicating of success stories and organizational goals are paramount to success. Six Sigma vision, goals, objectives, and corporate measures must be communicated by top management.

Other key performance measures are those that need to be developed or monitored (if in place) for key processes—operational and support. Operational processes are those that produce the company's products and services. Support processes are human resources, financial, legal, and administrative, and so forth. To improve processes, metrics are a must. They help identify where the problem is (they show the gap between where you are and where you want to go),

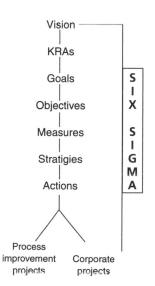

Controlled costs	Failure costs
• Approval	• Internal failure
Inspection, testing, product quality audits.	Failures in manufacturing area, retesting costs, scrap, rework, failure analysis, and so on
• Prevention	• External failures
In process inspection and testing, new design reviews, process control education and training.	Includes warrant charges, complaint adjustments, returned material, complaint failure analysis.
TOTAL COPQ COSTS = Controlled Costs + Failure Costs	

Figure 1.7 Cost of poor quality (COPQ).

and once countermeasures are implemented, the measures show where improvement was achieved.

Measures are an integral part of the Six Sigma analysis. An important one is cost of poor quality (COPQ) (see Figure 1.7). In Six Sigma or any key improvement effort, COPQ is an important performance measure. Firms estimate that COPQs can cost from 15 percent to 40 percent of sales or budget (www.successthroughquality.com/six_sigma_quality htm). Cost reduction and quality cost focuses have reduced COPQ in many companies to 3 percent or less.

Companies often spend more controlled costs to reduce failure costs, especially external failures that result in major costs. "Cost $1 to prevent a problem, $10 to find it, and $100 to fix it."

Check or estimate your COPQ. If more than 3 percent of your sales or operating costs, consider a strategic initiative to reduce the total COPQ. Also, measurement is the second step in the Six Sigma problem-solving process.

SIX SIGMA DMAIIC (Design, Measurement, Analysis, Improvement, Implement & Control).
The DMAIIC definitions are explained below. This is the heart of Six Sigma. It is the problem-solving tool/technique.

1. Define—Identify processes that need improvement and define linkage of measures, process, and customer's experiences. Define what the problem is, including what, why, and how much.

2. Measurement—First, document and describe the process. A flowchart is a good method. Develop necessary measurements and estimate the process capability (helps prioritize the need for improvement and shows present quality levels). Turn defects, errors, and COPQ into profits/success. Indicator development, as described in Chapter 3, can be very useful in this step.

Cannot do unless you have good performance indicators

3. Analysis—Evaluate the performance measure to determine the amount of improvement possible to make the critical process improvements (CPI) world class or at least best in class. Process redesign is probable.

4. Improvement—Identify specific product characteristics that must be improved to achieve the performance and financial targets desired. Then, the characteristics are evaluated to determine the major sources of variation. Develop an improvement plan that includes high-priority projects or opportunities.

5. Implement—Implement the improvement plan. Overcome the barriers using forces pulling for and transit to the new process.

6. Control—Monitor the process and report improvements to management, process participants, and clients. Drive ownership, accountability, and integration into the daily work of the organization.

1.8 DIFFERENT LEVELS OF ORGANIZATION MAY HAVE SAME OR DIFFERENT INDICATORS

Different levels of an organization may have indicators/metrics that are different and may have some that are the same. The same metrics could have great, little, or no influence on various departments. To demonstrate this, let's take a president of a university, the football coach, and the football stadium manager. Let's focus strictly on the football program. The indicators selected are primarily from the president's level, but let's see whether there is linkage at the other two organizational levels (see Figure 1.8).

Objectives 1 and 2 are very important to the president. The football coach shares each of these, and his or her actions affect the indicators. The coach especially relates to

President	Football Coach	Stadium Manager
Objective 1: Make money—Metric is profit and also attendance	Same, but less important	Same impact
Objective 2: Students—Graduate Metric is percentage of athletes that graduate on time	Same	No impact
Objective 3: Go To Bowl—Metric is number of wins and losses and whether or not team goes to bowl	Same but more important	Some impact
Objective 4: Recruiting Top Athletes Metric is percentage Blue Chip	Same, but more important	Some impact

Figure 1.8 Different levels of organization and their objectives' relationships.

objectives 3 and 4. His future employment and salary depend on how well these objectives are accomplished. The stadium manager directly affects only one: profit (but has some relationship with objectives 3 and 4, which are key ones for the president and the university). All three have numerous other metrics to manage. The president must worry about faculty staffing, developing a high-quality curriculum, providing community support, and obtaining the university's total finances. The football coach needs to have great assistant coaches, good offensive and defensive plans, playing fields, game plans, and football schedules. The stadium manager worries about ticket takers, food and beverage shops, security, cleanliness of the stadium, and parking. Each of these three jobs could have metrics. All three persons work for the university and make major contributions to its mission and welfare. Each has major metrics that help them measure their performance and continuously improve their operations. Some key indicators (strategic, corporate) are the same for each. Other members of the university, such as head of security, teachers, and counselors, also contribute to these corporate indicators. They also have many other indicators that are particular or specific to their jobs and processes.

1.9 BEWARE INDICATORS THAT CAN BE MANIPULATED AND MISUSED

1.9.1 Beware Indicators That Can Be Misused

Unfortunately, managers have used metrics/indicators wrongly in many situations. They have demanded improvements without providing the resources and training for the employees. Employees continuously get banged over the head but are helpless to do anything about it. Often bonuses and recognition are not possible to achieve because of the unrealistic targets and because not even superhuman effort (work harder and harder) can produce the desired results. Management uses the indicators to bang the employees over the head. Instead of this management by fear, the same indicators can be used for improvement. If management changes its attitude, supports the employees, encourages improvement, and leads the effort, these measures can be used for improvement.

1.9.2 Beware Indicators That Can Be Manipulated (Being Good versus Looking Good)

Unfortunately, metrics can often be manipulated. When management communicates to employees an important metric with a stretch target (goal), the employees are going to strive to reach it. Some employees will study the metric and if it is possible to manipulate it, they will. The word spreads and soon the metric's target is falsely achieved. "They asked for it and we gave it to them!" The "we versus them" philosophy kicks in.

One utility set a target (95 percent on time or ahead schedule) for customers' required dates for electrical construction to be met. The percentage complete was very low (approximately 25 percent) at the time the metric with targets was communicated. The schedulers at the service center working with the service planners found out they could get together and back-date things so that the target is always achieved. Soon all five divisions and more than 30 service centers showed 100 percent completion of customer service dates. Then the metric meant nothing and unfortunately no real improvement resulted. The correction to this situation can often be used as an example to stop manipulation.

1.9.2.1 Techniques for Minimizing Manipulation, Using Customers' Required Dates as an Example
First, the operational definition of what data are to be collected should be made very specific and parameters for collecting data should be set. The definition is made tight so no one can misinterpret what should or should not be included.

Second, an action plan is developed to include a process and countermeasures so that the metric will improve. If needed, the employees are to be trained in this method. Often they will discover it is easier to make improvements than it is to manipulate the metric. This was the case in the manipulation of customers' required dates.

Third, top management communicated that they knew that manipulations were happening and wanted it stopped right away. Manipulation stopped. Training occurred and real progress was made. The process and metric are still being used in the company more than 15 years later. Customer satisfaction has increased significantly. If manipulation doesn't stop, punitive action may be required.

1.10 FAILURE MODES

Here are the 11 most frequent reasons why indicators fail:

1. Definitions are not clear/boundaries are not established.

2. Management sends out wrong message (chases wrong rabbits).

3. Indicators are misunderstood (no buy-in).

4. Indicators are misused (control, comparisons when not applicable, "whipping stick").

5. Indicator takes additional time and reporting effort. As soon as possible, efforts stop.

6. Indicator not created here or by me (new boss).

7. Indicator not kept current (top problem) (sends the message management or supervisors do not care).

8. Targets are not realistic.

9. A flood of indicators results and no one reviews them because it is too many (key indicators gets lost in the crowd).

10. Indicators are not visible to those of interest.

11. Indicators are not calculated in time to be of value.

One book reviewer pointed out an excellent example. The entire workforce had been transferred or laid off and the quality assurance department posted month-old defect data on an empty factory floor. You can imagine how this was received by management.

Following chapters will outline procedures, methods, and techniques that will minimize the chance for failure.

Successful endeavors using metrics and communicating positively in conferences, publications, and books can encourage use and encourage management to look out for the failure modes and prevent them from occurring.

A measurement failure modes effects analysis (FMEA) can help identify failure modes for each objective and help determine the critical effort (1 to 5, with 5 being most critical). Root causes can be identified and countermeasures developed to eliminate or minimize their impact (see Figure 1.9 for a possible measurement FMEA).

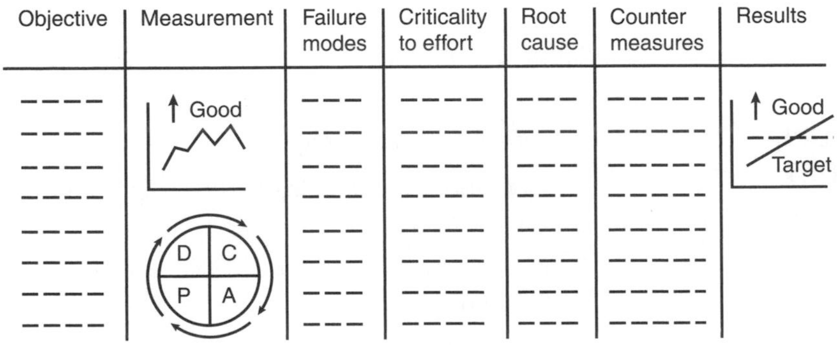

Figure 1.9   Measurement FMEA.

1.11 LEAN MEASUREMENT

Most companies have either too many measures or too few. Seldom would a measurement audit or evaluation result in finding just the right number and the proper ones.

When a company has too many measures, a lot of extra time and other resources are expended that add no value, resulting in waste. The elimination of this waste is what lean measures depict. Having the right metrics at the right place (process inputs, process itself, process outputs, and outcomes) at the right time is a goal worth pursuing.

When there are insufficient measures, resources are lost because there is little warning of potential problems, process corrections are not made when needed, strategic objectives are not implemented and monitored, and other waste occurs.

A measurement adds value only when it is important, monitored, and corrected if not trending as desired.

2

Management by Metrics

2.1 OBJECTIVES

1. Understand how metrics can be used in a system to improve organizational performance, process improvement, and project performance.

2. Understand the key elements of developing a strategic plan and their relationships.

3. See how metrics are an integral part of strategic planning and an organizational planning and measurement system.

2.2 GLOSSARY

BOATS—Acronym for business objectives attainment tracking system. BOATS is a technique that can be used by large organizations, with multiple objectives, to periodically assess the progress toward project milestones and obtaining results from countermeasures.

environmental scan—An intensive look at the future to see what is coming toward an organization from government, technology, environment, competition, and customers' needs. It is written and considered in developing issues.

key result areas (KRAs)—The areas of a company that, if emphasized and if resources are applied, will produce favorable results, including increased organizational performance and enhanced customer satisfaction.

key performance indicators (KPIs) or key success indicators (KSIs)—Methods that define and measure an organization's progress toward meeting its goals.

management review—A review produced when the key executives, directors, or managers (depending on organization level) convene periodically and address strategic measures, tactical measures, key processes measures, and project measures. If the targets are not being met, the managers address what needs to be done.

metric-based managed system—An organizational system in which strategic plan, corporate objectives, key processes, and strategic projects are measured and action is taken when goals or targets are not being met.

mission—What the business or organization was formed to accomplish. The functions that are done.

SMART objectives—When an objective is specific, measurable, actionable, relevant and realistic, and time-framed. Normally, an organization develops an objective then changes it to meet the SMART conditions.

SWOT analysis—Identification of strengths, weaknesses, opportunities, and threats. The analysis consists of matching strengths to overcome weaknesses or reduce threats. Also, it uses strengths to grasp opportunities for performance breakthrough.

2.3 METRICS-BASED MANAGEMENT SYSTEM/ ORGANIZATIONAL PLANNING AND MEASUREMENT

- Customer's voice
- Benchmarking
- Strategic planning

No

Yes

It is inconceivable that a world-class organization exists without a metrics-based management system. Metrics enable organizations to know where they are, assess the need for improvement, improve, and then monitor processes to ensure that they are under control and producing desired levels of quality.

Organizational planning develops the strategies that provide breakthrough improvements. These strategies will improve the corporate performance measures or metrics significantly, by 30 percent to 50 percent over one to three years.

Several tools and techniques help achieve the strategy development and execution process. First, companies measure customers' satisfaction and their expectations and use this information to develop strategic initiatives that will dramatically improve key processes. Benchmarking can also help identify possible strategies and improvements.

Strategic planning is the primary process for developing the strategies. The customers' voice and benchmarking enable this process. The essential parts are developing a vision (what you want to become); identifying your strengths, weaknesses, opportunities, and threats; and driving the strengths to overcome weaknesses and exploring opportunities, goals, objectives, and strategies.

Alignment or linkage gets all the vectors going in the same direction. It facilitates departments/functions/groups of people focused on what is important to the company or organization. Otherwise, it is common for the departments/functions to go their own way. The vectors then go in all directions.

That is why alignment is important. It ensures that all parts of an organization have priorities and/or activities that support the corporate strategies. This prevents waste and duplication of efforts while increasing the probability that major improvements can be achieved.

Some key organizational thrusts that save money:

- Alignment
- Accountability
- Process management and measurement
- Team and project measurements

Accountability helps everyone know what is important. Ensuring that jobs are properly designed and that people are adequately trained or competent in their jobs, and then holding people accountable, can add significant value to any organization. Measures at corporate, department, process, and job levels help keep the focus on what is important and show whether there are positive results. The measures provide the means to correct problems, eliminate bottlenecks, identify successes and their causes, and get or keep things moving in the right direction.

Processes are where the people work and the products or services are produced. Good performance measures for the processes help gauge how things are going, whether process is meeting its requirements, and whether corrective action is needed. They can facilitate increasing or decreasing production. Excellent process management is a must for any organization intending to become best in its class or world class.

Supplier management, ensuring that supplies provide value to the organization or company, is a highly beneficial endeavor. Measurement helps by gauging the supplier's performance.

Project or team initiatives need performance indicators to measure both progress and results. These measures should be put in place at the beginning and periodically reviewed to ensure that their purposes are being achieved.

Leadership is paramount to drive improvement, maintain the gains, and produce world-class products and services. Education and training are also essential in ensuring overall organizational excellence.

Business process management is essential (see Figure 2.1). Measures enable us to know how the processes are going, where we need improvement, and where we leave things as they are. When improvements are needed, projects are identified and teams formed. Measures guide them to improvements, and the results are visible after implementation.

"If you don't measure, how do you know if you improve?"

2.4 STRATEGIC PLANNING, ALIGNMENT, AND LINKAGE

2.4.1 Strategic Planning: The Mechanism for Breakthrough Performance

2.4.1.1 Mission/Vision
Strategic planning is the mechanism for achieving breakthrough performance. Once the first plan is accomplished, it should be revisited every year and not just for cosmetic purposes. It may need a complete makeover. There are numerous books on strategic planning processes, so an

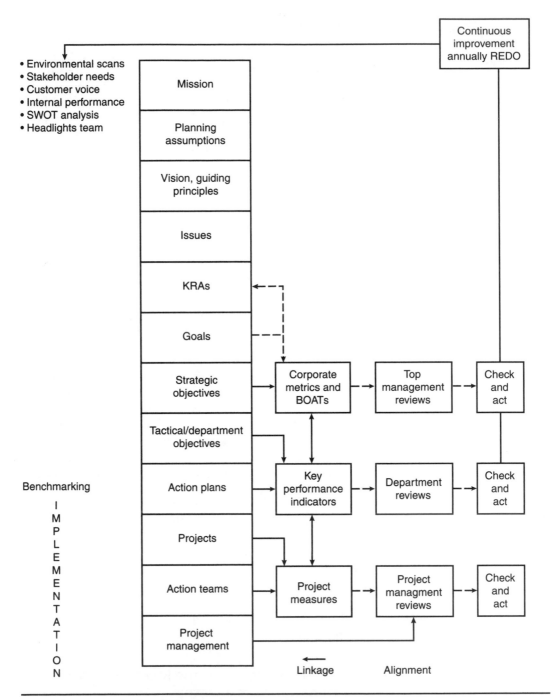

Figure 2.1   Organizational planning and measurement system.

exhaustive explanation here is not warranted. The key to effective strategic planning is to be sure all key players are included (preferably at an off-site location for the planning session); an environmental scan, to assess what's coming from government (federal and state), competition, and customers is completed before the planning session. Customer satisfaction measurements and comments should be considered in the planning session. The mission of the organization should be updated and a long-range vision of where the company wants to go should be updated or developed. Identify guiding principles and organizational values. The team should develop a SWOT (strengths, weakness, opportunities, threats) analysis. Using these tools, corporate issues should be identified. Headlight teams (smaller groups of participants) may be engaged in developing issues and opportunities and then each brought back to the session to present their findings. Opportunities from the SWOT and strengths (where the organization is strong) should be highlighted and become part of the recommendations.

Key result areas should be identified and turned into broad, long-range goals. For each goal, at least one SMART objective should be developed. SMART means specific, measurable, actionable, relevant or realistic, and time-framed. SMART will be addressed further in this chapter.

Identify your key result areas, which come from your mission and what you offer to your customers. These will facilitate goal setting and developing corporate initiatives and strategic measures. Converting KRAs into long-range goals becomes easy. With goals, established objectives can be determined. Making them SMART objectives facilitates measurement. Because of the importance of KRAs and the SMART concept, they will be further explained later. Corporate metrics that need to be improved to meet objectives, goals, and vision will need to be identified or developed.

Nine simplified diagrams will demonstrate each product of the strategic planning process as to how it is developed and the relationships to other key products.

2.4.1.2 Key Result Areas

In developing strategic indicators, the areas of focus are needed to ensure that what is measured, if improved, achieves organizational objectives, goals, and vision. Normally, each organization has three to six focus areas, called key result areas (KRAs), depending on their mission and products or services provided. If an organization focuses its resources on these areas, it will improve the organization's performance. FedEx, for example, focuses on people, service, and profit. Florida Power and Light focuses on quality, delivery, cost, safety, and corporate responsibility. Mercury Insurance focuses on service, security, and people. Most of the time these remain the same but are sometimes refined as time passes.

The key results areas are improvement thrusts, quality requirements, or priority areas. They are the areas that the

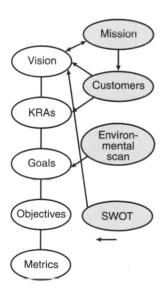

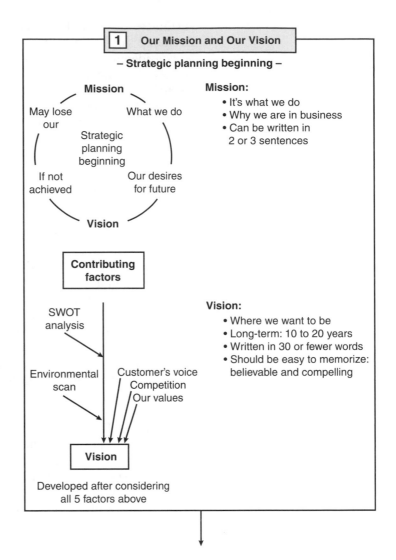

organization must succeed in to meet its strategic thrust. The author has identified 45 potential KRAs. Over 95 percent of organizations will find their KRAs are included on this list. Before identifying yours, ask, "What should our organization focus on to improve performance and customer satisfaction?" Once the KRAs are established, goals (broad and long-term) and objectives (short-term and specific) are developed by leadership or strategic council, and then metrics can be identified in support of these.

Let's review: The goals can be written using the KRAs as the basic thrust. Then at least one objective for each goal should be written using the SMART method in its development. This method facilitates measurement development.

In identifying the KRAs, the facilitator should:

1. Explain what a KRA is (what our customers receive when our organization performs our mission, and what our organization perceives as important).

2. Go over multivoting.

   Step 1. The first time, everyone gets to pick their 23 choices (approximately half of the total). After one choice is not selected, it cannot be selected in a future round. Vote and put the results on an easel with pad. Go over each of the 45 and annotate the votes each got.

   Step 2. Next, select from the highest vote getters (circle them) the ones you want participants to vote on next.

   Step 3. Vote again and repeat steps 1 and 2 until a vote gets to six possible KRAs.

   Step 4. Open up to discussion and ask for comments on each one. Is this a keeper? Do we need to add one more of the high vote getters (from last multivote) to our list? Try not to have more than seven, with four to five preferred.

   Step 5. Most of the time customer satisfaction is one of the KRAs selected. It should not be included, because all the other KRAs selected have as their first priority achieving high customer satisfaction. It is included so this extremely important point comes across. Now, open discussion and use criteria (such as appropriateness, coverage, and effectiveness) to help select the final four to eight.

2.4.1.3 Goals

Goals are long-range and broad. To turn a KRA into a goal, you only need to add an "action word." For example, let's take a few of the KRAs and turn them into possible goals.

KRA	Goal
Security	Improve security
Communications	Enhance communications
Productivity	Increase productivity
Quality	Focus on quality
Efficiency	Efficient application
Profit	Increase profits
Service	Improve service

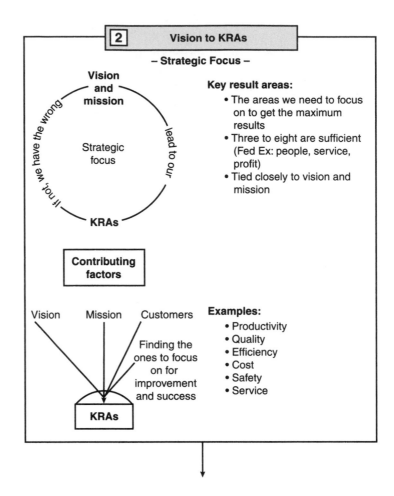

Also, some explanation is often done, such as, "Our customers feel secure in their investment," or, "Enhance communications to our customers and our employees."

2.4.1.4 SMART Objectives

The acronym means:

Smart

Measurable

Actionable

Reviewed and Realistic

Time-framed

Extra time is spent on developing the objectives using this concept, but it will actually save time in that the measures become evident for each objective.

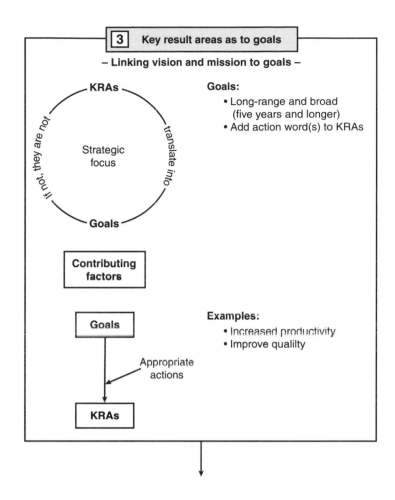

Let's look at two not-SMART objectives and then at the objectives rewritten as SMART ones.

Wrong: Institute pollution prevention in the Air Force.

Right: By end of 2006, develop and institute a pollution prevention program that will decrease waste by 20 percent.

Wrong: Increase our staffing assistance to the plants.

Right: Increase our in-person staffing assistance to the plants by 20 percent during next three years while maintaining our customer satisfaction rating at 4.2 or higher.

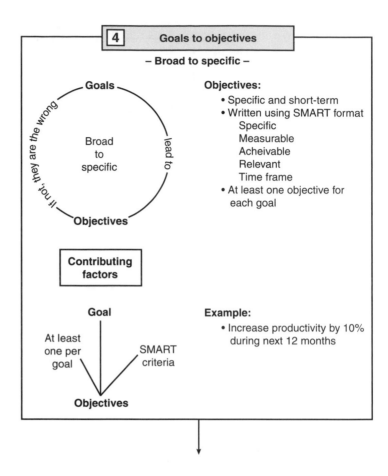

Metric: Percent on-site staff assistance. This is a process metric.

Metric: Customer satisfaction rating. This is an outcome metric.

Notice: The objective tells what we going to do, how much we desire to achieve, and in what time frame.

Check each of the above examples by asking questions for each letter (S, M, A, R, T):

Is this objective specific?
Is this objective measurable?
Is this objective actionable?
Is this objective realistic and relevant?
Is this objective time-framed?

If you get a "no" answer, determine what you need to do to make it a "yes." A SMART objective will have all "yes" answers. This procedure will not only provide you with excellent objectives that are actionable but also provide the measure and target for your indicator or metric.

Once objectives are established, action plans and teams are formed. Developing the plans is exciting and fun. However, implementation sometimes becomes a slow process because key players are so involved in their jobs and subject to the daily pressures encountered in the workplace. After experiencing this in numerous organizations, the author developed a metric (BOATS) that measures the percentage of a month's activities/events that are actually accomplished and one that reflects overall results. This keeps the champions and teams focused on continuous progress. In developing these metrics (one process and one results), a process is followed and includes management reviews. This process will be covered later in this chapter.

2.4.1.5 Strategies/Measure

Strategies are the specific initiatives used to achieve the objectives and impact favorably the corporate measures. For example, in the electric utility business, service reliability to its customers is generally measured by service unavailability or SAIDI (system average interruption duration index). The formula is complex in that it has several components.

$$\sum_{i}^{n} = 1 \; \frac{CI_i \cdot Duration_i}{C.\,S.} \; \text{where}$$

- CI is the number of customers interrupted

- Duration is the time the outage or interruption lasted

- C.S. is the total system customers served

- $\sum_{i}^{n} = 1$ is the sum of each interruption (n)

Strategies could consist of reducing the number of interruptions and reducing the number of customers interrupted for any interruption that could occur.

Reducing the time (duration) for interruptions and increasing the number of customers served are possible strategies that would affect the corporate metric, SAIDI. To improve SAIDI, countermeasures would have to be developed (probably by project teams or problem-solving teams) and implemented.

The following shows some possible countermeasures.

Strategy	Possible countermeasure
Reduce number of interruptions	• Reduce amount of small electric wire • Improve lightning arresters • Better maintenance

Strategy	Possible countermeasure
Reduce number of customers interrupted	• Additional fusing • Reduce load where possible (fewer customers on a lateral or feeder section)
Reduce duration time	• Reduce travel time • Faster restoration technique • Better staging of trouble trucks
Increase customers served	• Customer growth • Increase area served

Two important metrics to assist management in deploying objectives and reviewing them for progress will be developed and demonstrated.

2.5 BOATS (Business Objectives Attainment Tracking System)

BOATS is designed to propel or steer momentum and implementation of strategic objectives (see Figure 2.2). Therefore, before using BOATS-P, a vision must be developed, goals and objectives established, and metrics identified. The P stands for Process.

If these actions/developments have been done, the seven-step process can be effectively used (see Figure 2.3).

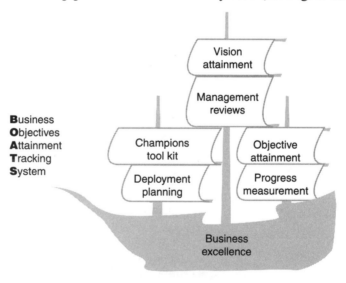

Figure 2.2   BOATS (Business Objectives Attainment Tracking System).

2.5.1   What Is It?

- A planning system that enables efficient deployment and implementation and achieves results.
- Two indicators that if reviewed monthly can reveal how effectively the Business Plan or Strategic Plan is being deployed and progress made to achieve it.
- An action plan and implementation plan that provides a roadmap to objective attainment.

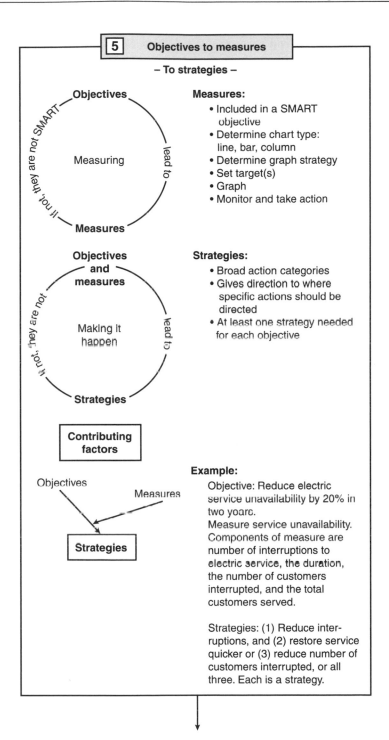

| 5 | Objectives to measures |

– To strategies –

Objectives

Measuring

Measures

If not, they are not SMART

lead to

Measures:
- Included in a SMART objective
- Determine chart type: line, bar, column
- Determine graph strategy
- Set target(s)
- Graph
- Monitor and take action

Objectives and measures

Making it happen

Strategies

If not, they are not

lead to

Strategies:
- Broad action categories
- Gives direction to where specific actions should be directed
- At least one strategy needed for each objective

Contributing factors

Objectives

Measures

Strategies

Example:

Objective: Reduce electric service unavailability by 20% in two years.

Measure service unavailability. Components of measure are number of interruptions to electric service, the duration, the number of customers interrupted, and the total customers served.

Strategies: (1) Reduce interruptions, and (2) restore service quicker or (3) reduce number of customers interrupted, or all three. Each is a strategy.

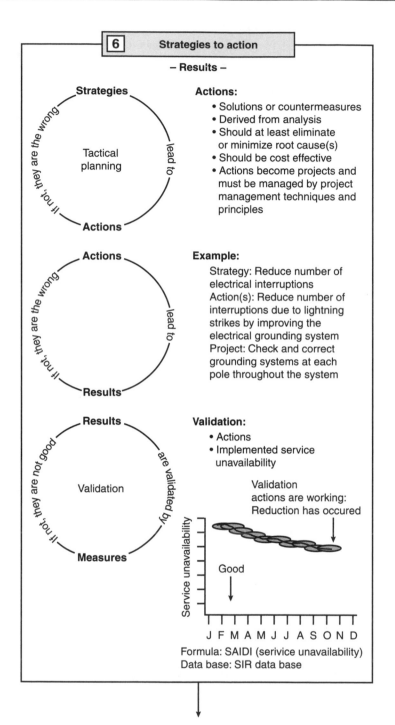

6   **Strategies to action**

– Results –

Strategies

If not, they are the wrong

Tactical planning

lead to

Actions

Actions:
- Solutions or countermeasures
- Derived from analysis
- Should at least eliminate or minimize root cause(s)
- Should be cost effective
- Actions become projects and must be managed by project management techniques and principles

Actions

If not, they are the wrong

lead to

Results

Example:
Strategy: Reduce number of electrical interruptions
Action(s): Reduce number of interruptions due to lightning strikes by improving the electrical grounding system
Project: Check and correct grounding systems at each pole throughout the system

Results

If not, they are not good

Validation

are validated by

Measures

Validation:
- Actions
- Implemented service unavailability

Validation actions are working: Reduction has occured

Service unavailability

Good

J F M A M J J A S O N D

Formula: SAIDI (serivice unavailability)
Data base: SIR data base

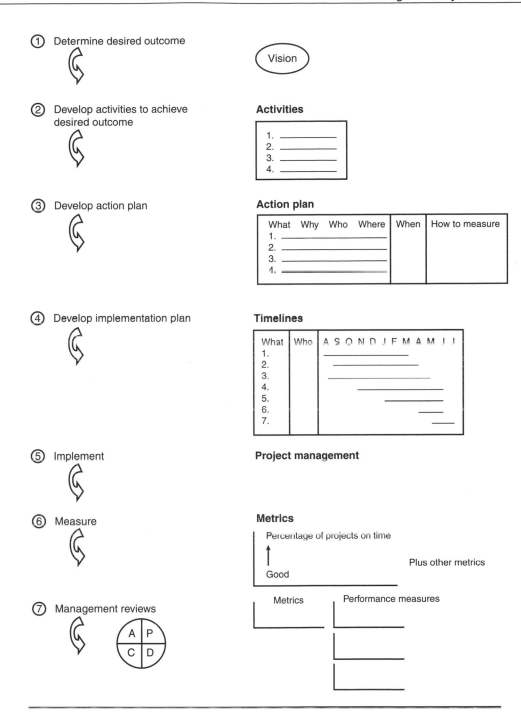

Figure 2.3 BOATS process steps.

It is wise to recognize a champion for each objective. Each champion is accountable for his or her objective's achievement. Normally, a champion is an executive and the objective (processes) functions falls mostly in his or her functional area. The champion appoints a team based on the members' knowledge, past performance, motivation, and availability.

If the strategic objectives are accomplished, the goals will be reached. If the goals are achieved, the vision will be realized. BOATS tells us:

- How are we doing in implementing our business objectives?

- Where are we having problems?

- What milestones were not met?

- What directorates and divisions are on schedule and which are achieving results?

2.5.2 BOATS Process

Figure 2.3 shows the seven steps of the BOATs process. The first step is determining the desired outcome. Doing this enables you to ask, "What does it take to achieve this outcome?" The following shows these two steps. Desired outcome helps us know how we are doing on implementing our strategic plan objectives.

Individual projects will have different activities. For example, to develop a publication, the activities may be 1. identify the topic; 2. research the Web; 3. research the library; 4. interview key individuals; 5. develop outline; 6. write; 7. review and edit; 8. publish. The desired outcome may be "enlighten company personnel on corporate values and our guiding principles."

Your objective project:

The champion and strategic objective team review their objective and ask, "What do we hope to achieve?" The recorder lists the possibilities as the team and champion brainstorm. After the list is exhausted, the key outcomes are marked and then written in clear form.

Example 1:

Goals—Improve Safety

Objective: Decrease accidents by 10 percent by end of year 2007.

Desired Outcomes Established

- Truck and other vehicle accidents reduced.
- Office accidents reduced.
- Every employee received safety training.
- All supervisors emphasized safety awareness.
- Weekly safety meetings held.
- Recognition of good safety records.
- All accidents are recorded; cause-and-effect analysis is performed on each.
- Employees are kept informed of progress, problems, and new opportunities for improvement.

Example 2:

Goals—Improve Quality of the Call Center Operations

Objective: Increase customer satisfaction by 50 percent.

Desired Outcomes Established

- When customers call, the call center answers the phone in three rings or sooner.
- Customers receive accurate answers.
- When problem is being worked on, customer is involved in the process until decision and conclusion are achieved.
- Improvements are sought from the customers and implemented when feasible.
- Attitude that customer is "number 1" prevails in all calls answered.
- The call center members are fully trained in all products/services available and can speak clearly about them.
- Members learn to handle difficult calls and turn them into satisfying experiences.
- Customer's perceptions should be one of caring, competent, and customer-oriented employees.

The strategic objective team puts the desired outcomes in a place visible to all team members. Next, one of two methods works effectively. The first method is to ask what do we need to do first, then second, and so on. List the activities, adding and changing as necessary, until the complete list of activities has been identified. The second method, normally used by an experienced facilitator, is to flowchart the process required to achieve the desired outcomes. Ask what do we need to do first, who does it, what comes next, and so on, until all key activities and events are identified and placed under the heading Who Accomplishes. The flowchart should give you what needs to be done and who does each activity.

2.5.3 Action Plans

Action plans show what we are going to do, why we are doing it, who is going to do it, where it is going to be accomplished, when it will be done, and how you know when it has been completed. Figure 2.4 shows an example of a completed action plan. The action plan is used to develop the implementation plan (see following example). Sometimes, only one plan is developed that incorporates a little of both, and it is normally called an action plan.

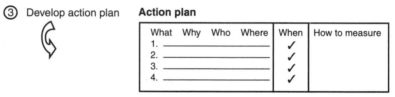

What are the activities?

2.5.4 Develop Implementation Plan and Implement

Developing an implementation plan is relatively easy after the action plans have been completed (see previous example). Basically, the implementation plan takes the activities and person or department responsible and shows when each activity will start and finish.

Before implementation, the plan and the resources must be approved by the budget or resource team or committee

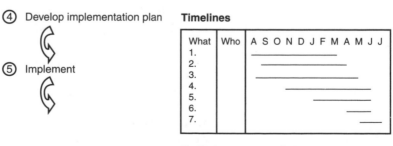

Project management

Goal 1: Provide the leadership and vision to move this organization smoothly and effectively to world-class performance and customer satisfaction.

Objective 2: Develop methodology by 31 Dec 2005 to ensure resources are balanced against mission requirements to maximize our efficiency and effectiveness in meeting changing and increasing work requirements. Champion IT Vice President

Desired Outcome: Achieve proper balance of dollars and people by account and by Directorate and product line.

What	Why	How	Who	When	Measures
1. Establish objective	To improve workload capability and effectiveness	• Strategic planning process	• Leadership council	• 5 Mar 05	• Included or not
2. Appoint champion	To provide cross-functional management and leadership	• Process owner • Volunteer	• Leadership council	• Mar 05	• Accomplished or not
3. Develop approach	To deploy objective	• Brainstorming and discussing with resources chief	• Champion	• 16 May 05	• Develop or not
4. Determine gap	Identify improvement opportunities	• Gap analysis	• Champion, resource Division chief and budget	• 2 Jun-31 Jul 05	• Completed or not
5. Develop counter-measures	To improve and meet the objective	• Idea evaluated as to feasibility, suitability effectiveness	• Champion, resource Division chief and budget	• 4-29 Aug 05	• Completed or not
6. Implement	To achieve objective	• Financial working group process modified	• Financial working Group/Bgt Res. Div	• 1-30 Sept 05	• Process changed or not
7. Assess directors perception of Improvement	To see if improvement was achieved or if new measures should be taken	• Interviews or survey	• Champion • QI assist	• Periodically Nov 05, Jan or Feb 06 QC Mtg	• Satisfaction with results
8. Monitor, take action if needed	To check/study how things are going	• QC perception	• Champion/QI	• Ongoing	• See 7 above

Figure 2.4 Strategic plan 2005: Action plan.

(or organization in your company with budget approval). The objective champion should ensure that the objective team has identified resources needed, cost/benefits analysis when practical, force field analysis, and so on.

The tasks/activities needed are determined, and who will accomplish each is annotated. Next, the time frame of when it will start and finished is assessed. Any significant events, resources, and notes are annotated on the plan. Milestones can be shown and actual versus plan can be reflected.

2.5.5 The Measures: BOATS P & R

Figure 2.6 shows the BOATS-P metric, percentage of activities completed on or ahead of schedule. *P* stands for process (See Figure 2.5.)

A. Number remarks	B. What (Tasks/activities)	C. Who	D. When J F M A M J J A S O N D	E.

Figure 2.5   Implementation plan.

Figure 2.7 shows an example of calculating the monthly figures to plot on the graph.

For corporate measures on strategic initiatives, a composite monthly indicator that graphs the percentage of the indicators that meet or exceed the targeted amount can be helpful. It is a BOATS-R (*R* stands for results) metric and should be reviewed monthly by management. If a problem exists, peel back to the individual corporate indicators to find the problem.

For May, the percentage would be (cost-no, schedule-yes, safety-no, quality-no) 25 percent (1 out of 4).

For large corporations, the BOATS-R metric should be one of the primary elements included in the corporation's president's and senior or executive vice president's incentive plan. Senior and executive VPs have responsibility for more than one functional area. The VPs of functional areas need to manage their BOATS-P and BOATS-R metrics and be held accountable to the process and targets. Their incentives ought to include how they impacted the corporate measures, especially the ones they have the most possibility of impacting.

This composite indicator is good to go along with the activity measure (BOATS-P). This indicator measures results. Figure 2.8 shows several methods to impact corporate measures. Strategic planning, Six Sigma, benchmarking, and process reengineering are four major methods. Problem-solving teams, process improvements, and lean methods can carry out the four methods.

For example:

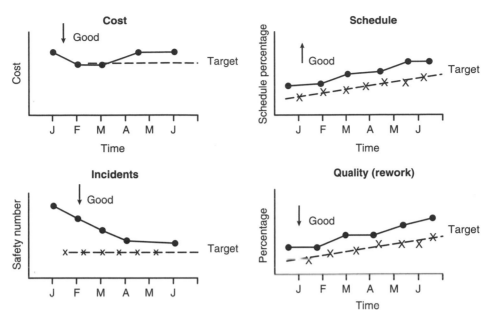

For the month of May, the percentage would be
(Cost – no, Schedule – yes, Safety – no, Quality – no) or 25% (1out of 4).

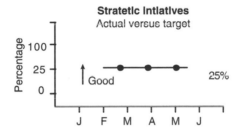

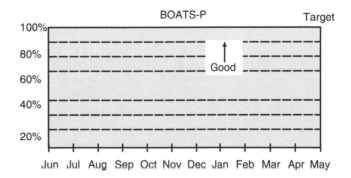

Updated monthly. Data received from Champions from their implementation plan — actual versus planned

Figure 2.6 Percentage of activities completed on or ahead of schedule.

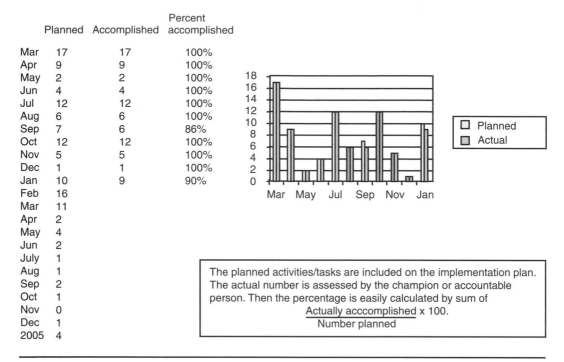

	Planned	Accomplished	Percent accomplished
Mar	17	17	100%
Apr	9	9	100%
May	2	2	100%
Jun	4	4	100%
Jul	12	12	100%
Aug	6	6	100%
Sep	7	6	86%
Oct	12	12	100%
Nov	5	5	100%
Dec	1	1	100%
Jan	10	9	90%
Feb	16		
Mar	11		
Apr	2		
May	4		
Jun	2		
July	1		
Aug	1		
Sep	2		
Oct	1		
Nov	0		
Dec	1		
2005	4		

The planned activities/tasks are included on the implementation plan. The actual number is assessed by the champion or accountable person. Then the percentage is easily calculated by sum of

$$\frac{\text{Actually acccomplished}}{\text{Number planned}} \times 100.$$

Figure 2.7 Percentage of objectives completed on time.

2.5.6 Management Reviews/Results

The management review team consists of top management whose job it is to review progress, take corrective action when needed, provide resources, and recognize and award high performances of individuals and teams.

During the top management reviews, the process BOATS-P metric is the first performance indicator presented and discussed. If it is going well, implementation is on track. If not, the champions of the objective are asked to explain what is the problem, what is being done about it, and whether top management can help in any way to get it back on track. Next, the BOATS-R metric, the corporate indicators/strategic metrics, is reviewed for status and trends, progress, problems, need for resources, and bottlenecks. Without conducting these reviews at least quarterly, the management emphasis, support, and leadership commitment suffers significantly. These reviews ensure that all the vectors are in alignment and results are being achieved. The results display is shown on page 41. Results come from improvement efforts and by managing these actions/projects to completion.

Next, project management is covered. Managing projects to efficiently and effectively achieve the objectives is a must.

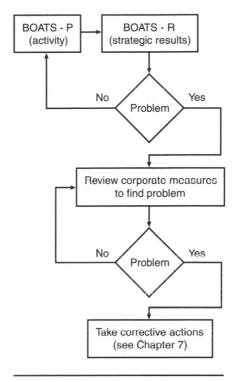

Figure 2.8 Composite indicator.

2.5.7 Project Management

In strategic planning, process reengineering, or major process improvement, takes projects and resources. Project management is a technique that enables a team or an organization to focus on implementation, ensuring that the budget and schedule are adhered to throughout.

The project management model is on page 42. Project management functions and activities include coordination; monitoring; reviewing milestones, activities, and schedule; and taking corrective action when necessary. The main focus is normally on bringing the project in on budget and on schedule, but quality, safety, and other key result areas could also be part of the process because of their high importance. No large facility or plant is built today without the help of project management. Even on small team projects, project management principles and tools should be used to meet time-frame and cost guidelines.

Next, a series of events or actions that include determining vision, KRAs, goals, objectives, measures, strategies, results, management reviews, and then project management are outlined. Following these will enable any organization to become efficient and effective in the organizational planning and pursuit of excellence.

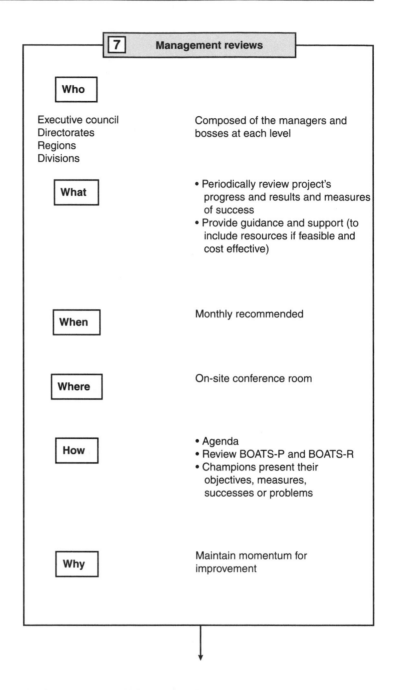

2.6 PERFORMANCE-BASED BUDGETING (A DIFFERENT TWIST TO STRATEGIC PLANNING)

Performance-based budgeting had its beginning in Sunnyvale, California. Mayor John Mercer implemented a performance-based budgeting system because costs and customers' requirements were increasing. He wanted a system to tie dollar resources to improvements sought. The city's costs went down, its service production up, and customer satisfaction significantly increased.

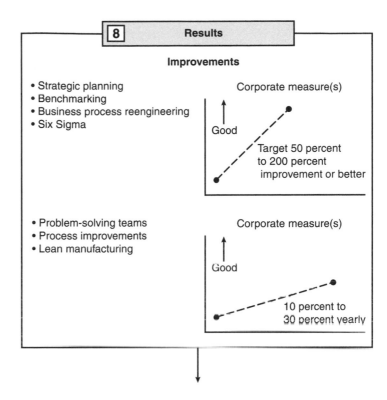

The system consisted of two plans: a strategic plan and an annual performance plan. The strategic plan consisted of a mission statement that shows clearly and specifically what the organization's purpose is, written in results-oriented fashion (see Figure 2.9).

From the mission statement, goals are developed (long-range and broad) and from them at least one objective was established. These objectives can be for more than a year's time. They should have performance measures that measure progress over time against the strategic objectives.

These performance goals are for one year's time, what is going to be accomplished that year. These are tied to the

Figure 2.9 Strategic plan.

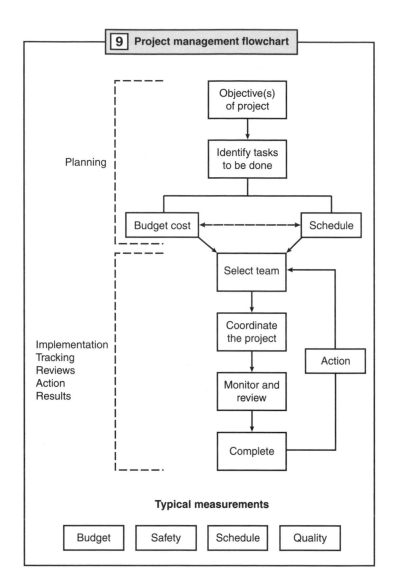

9 **Project management flowchart**

Planning

Objective(s) of project

Identify tasks to be done

Budget cost ←------→ Schedule

Select team

Implementation
Tracking
Reviews
Action
Results

Coordinate the project

Monitor and review

Action

Complete

Typical measurements

| Budget | Safety | Schedule | Quality |

budget: a budget account and a program activity. Each project activity is costed out and added together to determine total cost. Normally, an organization's accounting system has to be modified to do this.

The strategic plan and organizational plan model outlined can achieve (even better with a vision, KRAs, and smart objectives) the same results down to annual performance goals. Tying the improvement dollars to results is more difficult in that most organizations' budgets do not have the capability to track individual strategic projects. In government, the accounting system to do this is called a

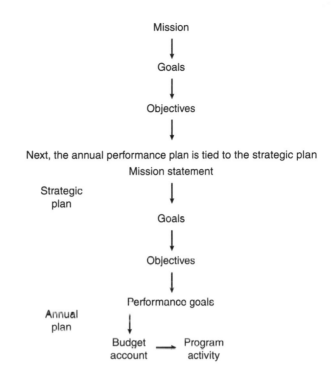

Mission

↓

Goals

↓

Objectives

↓

Next, the annual performance plan is tied to the strategic plan

Mission statement

Strategic
plan

↓

Goals

↓

Objectives

↓

Performance goals

Annual
plan

↓

Budget ⟶ Program
account   activity

managerial cost accounting system. In industry and government, similar results can be obtained if an ROR (rate of return) is accomplished for each project, budget committee approves each, and results are tracked and effectiveness and efficiency assessed annually.

3

Metric Development Process

3.1 OBJECTIVES

1. Understand that a process can be followed in developing meaningful performance indicators (PIs).

2. Know that good PIs don't just happen; most need to be developed.

3. Become familiar with tools and techniques to identify good measures.

4. Be able to evaluate PIs as to whether they are meaningful and useful.

5. Understand how to measure programs and corporate initiatives that go through stages of implementation.

3.2 GLOSSARY

brainstorming—A technique to generate a number of ideas by using a group of people and following a simple process. (See Appendix B.)

guiding principles—Established principles that a company or organization can follow to achieve the desired results (organization culture, values, performance).

nominal group technique (NGT)—A technique to generate ideas by a group using silent generation and to identify and prioritize possibilities. (See Appendix A.)

3.3 THE PROCESS FOR DEVELOPING STRATEGIC METRICS

Developing metrics is an art, not a science. Top management (leadership council, quality council, and so forth) plays a major role in developing strategic or corporate metrics. Figure 3.1 shows the process of developing the metric through construction of the performance indicator and setting targets. The roles/responsibilities are outlined for top management, the strategic objective champion, the team leader, team members, and department heads (see Figure 3.2).

Top leadership council   Champion   Team leader   Team members   Department heads

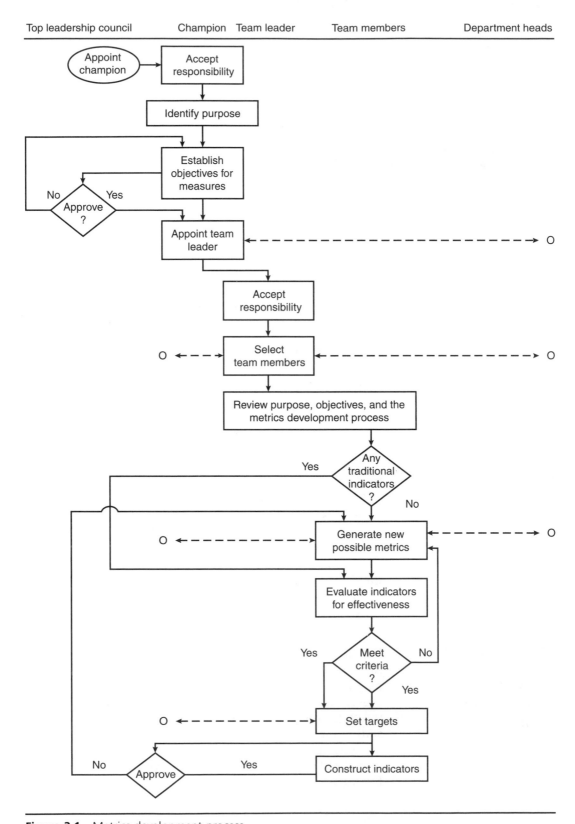

Figure 3.1 Metrics development process.

Top leadership council

- Develop strategic or business objectives
- Decide on need for a measure
- Identify champion
- Identify purpose
- Approve measurement objectives
- Approve new metrics or traditional metrics
- Conduct management reviews of metrics performance
- Approve resources for improvements
- Encourage continuous improvement
- Recognize and reward achievement

Champion

- Establish team
- Establish measurement objectives
- Follow metric development process
- Support team in resources (meeting places, time from job to do team duties, etc.)
- Keep top management informed of actions and status
- Obtain approvals from top management, when needed
- Assist in conducting management reviews

Team leader

- Select team members
- Manage team meetings and conflict
- Keep team on track
- Keep department managers and champion Informed of status, problems, and future plans
- Delegate responsibilities
- Recognize contributions
- Learn the process for developing performance indicators

Team members

- Assist team leader in following metric development process In developing indicator(s)
- Perform duties as assigned
- Develop indicator presentation format
- Participate in meetings and presentations

Department managers

- Provide team members requested (if possible, if not, offer satisfactory replacements
- Offer recommendations
- Manage the metrics and provide continuous improvement
- If the purpose is not strategic, then often the department head becomes the champion and does both jobs (champion and department head)

Figure 3.2 Roles/responsibilities.

3.4 THE PROCESS OF DEVELOPING PERFORMANCE INDICATORS, PROJECT INDICATORS, AND OTHER MEASURES

Depending on the location in the organization structure and the purpose of the metric, the process may vary from a team and a champion to a team with no champion or to an individual. However, the key steps in Figure 3.1 are still followed in developing the performance indicators. The seven steps are outlined in Figure 3.3.

---

1. Identify purpose and establish objectives(s). (Chapter 3)
2. Determine if existing traditional Indicators are available and are appropriate. (Chapter 3)
3. Generate new possible indicators. (Chapters 3 & 9)
4. Evaluate indicators for effectiveness. (Chapter 3)
5. Construct indicator graphs. (Chapter 4)
6. Select targets and plot on graph. (Chapter 5)
7. Monitor and act. (Chapters 6 & 7)

Figure 3.3 Metric development process.

3.4.1 Identify Your Purpose and Objective

The purpose should be aligned with the organization's mission, vision, goals, and objectives. They should consider customers' needs and serve as a foundation for accomplishing and sustaining continuous improvement.

The objectives should state how this metric will be used. Define the who, what, when, why, and how of this metric so that it can meet good indicator characteristics test. Repeatability, congruency, and consistency are assured in the metric. Specifically, the type of metric (supplier, process, output, outcome) should be annotated. What it measures and why should be clearly outlined.

3.4.2 Determine Whether Existing Indicators or Traditional Indicators Are Available and Are Appropriate

Check existing measures to determine adequacy. Next look for traditional indicators.

Often an industry or a function such as drafting or warehousing will already have indicators that have been in use for numerous years. Sometimes professional organizations capture the industry data and will share it with industry members. In the utility industry, seven well-known indicators, such as availability of electricity, service unavailability, interruptions to service, and momentary interruptions, are calculated monthly. However, because of competition in recent years brought on by possible deregulation, companies will not freely exchange the information. The same is occurring in hospitals and other service organizations. Manufacturers have always held their data as proprietary.

Libraries are a good source to research for traditional indicators. Benchmarking clearinghouses are another excellent source. An Internet search for benchmarking clearinghouses will provide you with several sources for your use. Some you will find are:

> Case Study Central—1000 benchmarks, best practices, surveys, articles, and so on. You can reach it at *www.bpir.com.*

> Clearinghouse Info—Free articles and clearinghouse information. *www.mywiseowl.com.*

> APQC (American Productivity and Quality Center)— An internationally recognized nonprofit organization that provides expertise in benchmarking and best-practices research. *apqcinfo@apqc.org, www.apqc.org,* 1-800-776-9676 or 1-713-687-4020.

> National Aeronautics and Space Administration—The Kennedy Space Center Benchmarking Clearinghouse, benchmarking.ksc.nasa.gov. Users can find links to other organizations such as APQC, The Benchmarking Exchange, and the Benchmarking Network.

> Asian Benchmarking Clearinghouse, Hong Kong Productivity Council. *www.abc.org.hk*

If an appropriate, traditional metric is found, a new one will not have to be generated. This will save time and effort, plus you will have one you know you can use to benchmark with other organizations.

Some generic indicators often used in strategic planning or organizational improvement efforts follow.

Financial	**Customers**
Sales	Retention
Profits	Satisfaction
Return on investment	Loyalty
Economical value added	Market share

Organizational outputs/outcomes

Response time

Throughput

Safety

Delivery on time

Productivity

Image/reputation

Cycle time

Process-per-million defect rates

Waste

Rework

Scrap

Process yield

Cost of poor quality

Construction

Schedule achievement

Cost/budget

Rework

Safety

Employees

Satisfaction

Retention

Productivity

Absenteeism

Suggestions submitted

Suggestions approved

Internal

Quality of work life

Budget

Efficiency

Utilization

Internal customer satisfaction

Cost avoidance/savings

Cash flow

Individual industries have their own.

3.4.3 Generate New Possible Indicators and Evaluate as to the Good Indicator Criteria

This is where few, if any, books on measurement provide the readers with "how to develop a new indicator." Normally, those books deal with traditional indicators or suggest that new ones just appear once you decide you need one. Unfortunately, this appearance act never happens unless a lot of thought and effort is put forth.

3.4.3.1 Method 1: Name implies unit of measure

Title ⟶ Title Method
For simple measures, this method works well. It is for measuring items, events, activities, and so on, that just in their name or title implies what should be measured.

1. Title ⟶ What is the objective? And how should we measure it? What should the units be (Y axis)? And what time periods (weeks, months, and so on) should we measure on X axis?

2. Title ⟶ Form of title

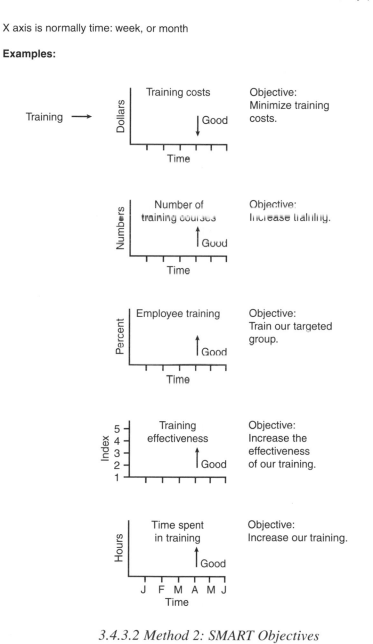

X axis is normally time: week, or month

Examples:

3.4.3.2 Method 2: SMART Objectives
Chapter 2 discussed SMART objectives. Once an objective is put in this format, the indicator and its target are included in the statement.

Increase sales by 50 percent during next three years.

Target is 50 percent by end of year 2006

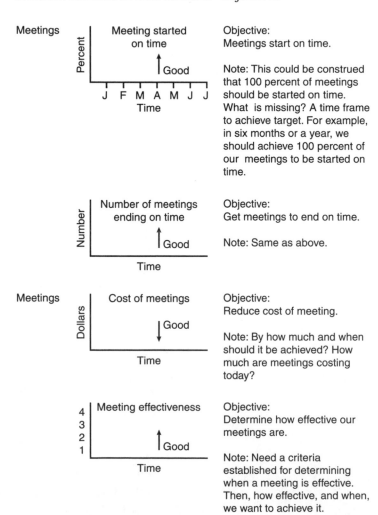

3.4.3.2.1 Method 2: Not SMART Objectives

Meetings

Meeting started on time

Percent

Good

J F M A M J J
Time

Objective:
Meetings start on time.

Note: This could be construed that 100 percent of meetings should be started on time. What is missing? A time frame to achieve target. For example, in six months or a year, we should achieve 100 percent of our meetings to be started on time.

Number of meetings ending on time

Number

Good

Time

Objective:
Get meetings to end on time.

Note: Same as above.

Meetings

Cost of meetings

Dollars

Good

Time

Objective:
Reduce cost of meeting.

Note: By how much and when should it be achieved? How much are meetings costing today?

Meeting effectiveness

4
3
2
1

Good

Time

Objective:
Determine how effective our meetings are.

Note: Need a criteria established for determining when a meeting is effective. Then, how effective, and when, we want to achieve it.

3.4.3.3 Method 3: Index

The scales come from surveys administered on a predetermined time (monthly, quarterly, and so forth). As you can see, there are several ways to measure the same subject title. It is important to always spell out why we are measuring this. What is our purpose or objective? Only then are we ready to design or develop the appropriate measures.

There are four general types of survey questions: the agreement scale (1–7), extent scale (1–7), satisfaction scale (1–7), and frequency scale (1–4).

Scales used for items included:

Agreement scale

1	2	3	4	5	6	7
Strongly disagree	Moderately disagree	Slightly disagree	Neither agree/disagree	Slightly agree	Moderately agree	Strongly agree

Extent scale

1	2	3	4	5	6	7
Not at all	To a very little extent	To a little extent	To a moderate extent	To a fairly large extent	To a great extent	To a very great extent

Satisfaction scale

1	2	3	4	5	6	7
Extremely dissatisfied	Moderately dissatisfied	Slightly dissatisfied	Neither sat/disat	Slightly satisfied	Moderately satisfied	Extremely satisfied

Frequency scale

1	2	3	4
Never	Occasionally	About half the time	All of the time

The indicator can be for one survey or several surveys. Additional column charts would show the different surveys. Percentage or scale can be used on the Y axis depending on what you want to emphasize.

How often are group meetings used to solve problems and establish objectives

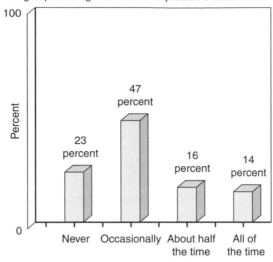

Comparison between two surveys

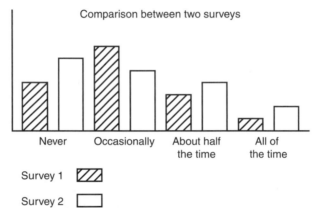

Survey 1 ▨

Survey 2 ☐

Using an extended scale of 1 to 7 gives us this result for the question:
To what extent are the leaders available?

Senior leadership access mean responses

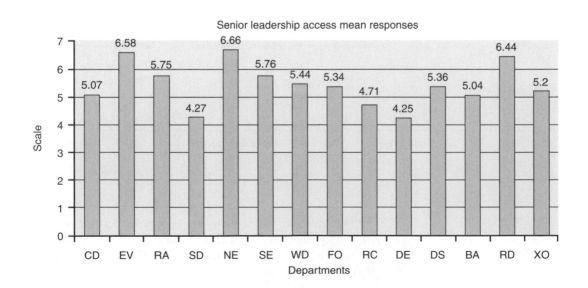

3.4.3.4 Method 4: Group Development: Using nominal group techniques or brainstorming

Step 1. Gather a group of four to six people knowledgeable about the subject.

Step 2. Use nominal group technique (see Appendix A) or brainstorming technique (see Appendix B). Write objective/goal/policy/problem so that everyone can see it. Generate factors that affect the objective (Sink, 1989).

Factors that impact

Improve electric service reliability

- Frequency of interruptions
- Amount of service unavailability
- Number of interruptions
- Time of interruptions
- Duration of interruptions
- Restoration process
- Traffic congestion
- Location of fault
- Number of customers affected
- Number of trouble men on duty
- How quickly the problem was called in
- Seriousness of interruption
- Equipment availability
- Storm or normal weather
- Material availability

Step 3. Are there any traditional indicators that can measure the improvement in electric service reliability? In this case, there are several and selecting one or two follows. If there were no traditional indicators, then these factors would be narrowed down to 3 to 5 by multivoting, and then one or two selected depending on how they met the indicator criteria.

3.4.3.5 Method 5: Structure Tree (What/how chart)

3.4.3.6 Method 6: Project Measures Development
The best way to develop project measures is to first flow-chart the activities. Then for each activity or event and related questions, ask whether something should be counted here or whether a measure would be valuable in providing

Step 1. What to measure, ask how, and write down potential measures.

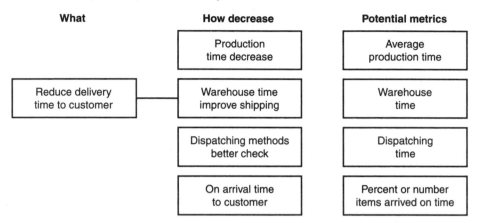

Step 2. Select one or two.

Step 3. Graph.

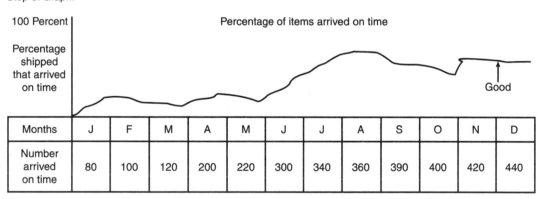

Months	J	F	M	A	M	J	J	A	S	O	N	D
Number arrived on time	80	100	120	200	220	300	340	360	390	400	420	440

information that can drive appropriate actions. (See eBay example, Chapter 7.)

For big projects such as major construction and large maintenance projects, a different approach may be helpful.

Critical success factors ⟶ Objectives ⟶ Measures

Critical success factors are those activities and events that must occur for the project to be very successful. The objectives should be in SMART format (see Chapter 3). Using the SMART objectives, it is relatively easy to identify the best performance measure(s). The flowchart is shown in Figure 3.4. All of the flowchart steps or activities are

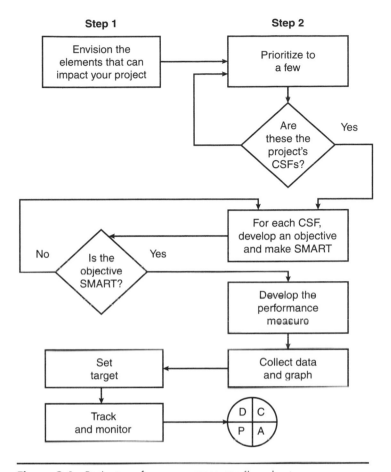

Figure 3.4 Project performance measures flowchart.

explained elsewhere in the book, but identifying the critical success factors has not.

Critical success factors (CSFs) are those characteristics, auditions, or variables that directly influence a customer's satisfaction with a specific business process and therefore influence the success of the entire business. The CSFs must receive satisfactory performance for any business to be successful. Examples include increased shareholder value, product quality, cost reduction manage commitment, projects, and measurement (APQC, 1993).

Envision the future for construction. There are more than 100 possible elements that can impact a major construction project. Categories include project controls, project rules, schedule, supervision, weather, contractors, and information. Let's get more specific.

Information

The accuracy of information supplied to the engineer by the owner.

Controls

The type of controls used on the project.

Schedule

How realistic the project schedule is.

Using brainstorming or nominal group technique, identify all major elements that could affect the project. Next have the management staff—construction manager, design, engineer, craft supervisors, and others—multivote the eight or 10 most important elements. These become the CSFs. Turn the CSFs into SMART objectives, and then the measures are evident.

CSF—A realistic project schedule.

Objective—Meet or beat the project scheduled during project life.

SMART objective—Improve construction performance and stay ahead of schedule during 2006.

Performance measure(s)—Schedule adherence = $\dfrac{\text{Actual man hours}}{\text{Planned man hours}}$

Earned Value = Percent project completed $\times$ budgeted amount

3.4.3.7 Method 7: Meeting Desired Outcomes

In this situation, you have a desired outcome but need to figure out how to achieve it. This is often true in large programs.

Step 1. Define the desired outcome.

Step 2. Determine the factor(s) that need to happen and their extent and time frame. If these happen then the desired outcome would be achieved.

This method was partially demonstrated on January 19, 2005, at Secretary of State Condoleezza Rice's confirmation hearing, conducted by the Foreign Relations Committee of the Senate.

Developing an exit strategy

The Big Issue—When can our troops come home? A timetable?

All agreed, Iraqis must be able to maintain stability and security with their own forces.

How would they do that? Answer: With trained native capable troops or policemen.

How many are trained now? Answer: 140,000 trained, says Rice.

Not so, says Senator Joe Biden. There are only 4000 who can really fight and be effective.

Questions came. What is the true number that are effective now? How are we going to measure? The chairman queried, "We need indicators of progress? Also, how many do we need for Iraq to maintain stability and security?"

When is an Iraqi trained to meet the requirements? Biden said, "When they can take the place of a U.S. soldier."

Rice disagreed. "When they have all the skills to handle the insurgency."

The desired outcome is for the United States to leave when Iraq is stable and secure.

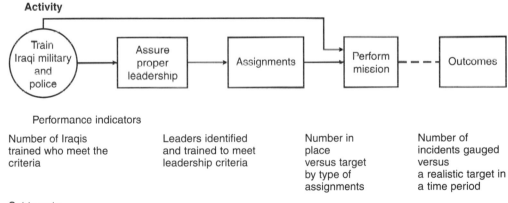

Activity

| Train Iraqi military and police | Assure proper leadership | Assignments | Perform mission | Outcomes |

Performance indicators

| Number of Iraqis trained who meet the criteria | Leaders identified and trained to meet leadership criteria | Number in place versus target by type of assignments | Number of incidents gauged versus a realistic target in a time period |

Set targets

The outcome indicator is the number of incidents that are realistic in a specified time period. Acceptable is inferred but not used because no incident is really ever acceptable. Therefore, U.S. leaders have an exit strategy measurement provided:

1. They (Congress) can determine when an Iraqi soldier or policeman is trained properly and ready to meet the mission.

2. They can arrive at a reasonable, mutually acceptable desired outcome.

3. The number of trained soldiers and policemen is the only factor needed to achieve the desired outcome.

Next, action plans to achieve the necessary training and measurement of the progress need to be put in place. Seldom is a matter of such importance quantified and published to the public. "We will stay the course until the job is done" is the prevailing strategy. When the job is done is left to interpretation.

3.4.3.8 Method 8: Selection of Lower-Level Measures as to Their Impact on Higher-Level Measures

Example, Six Sigma projects measures:

In the strategic focus, the change in sigma quality levels will probably be targeted.

Going from three sigma to six sigma in five years. For example: Specific Six Sigma projects will impact these strategic targets, but few changes will occur for an individual project. Maybe a change of 2.59 to 3.19 occurs. However, other performance measures that link to the strategic measures could show a lot of change and be more sensitive and motivating. They are defects per million (DPM), yield, and process capability (measured by Cpk-process capability ratio, which is the difference between upper and lower specification limits divided by 60 times the standard deviation).

For the change 2.59 sigma to 3.19 sigma, let's look at DPM and yield. They change as follows:

	2.59 sigma	3.19 sigma
DPM	137,097	45,500
Yield	86.2%	95.43%

With the small change in sigma quality level, there is a significant decrease in DPM of 91,597 and a 10.7 percent increase in yield.

The Cpk (process capability) changes will show whether the process is now in control or not and how close you are to being in control if you are not.

The DFM is indeed a good actionable measure along of course with process capability. Yield is another. In this example DPM decreased by 91,597 and the yield by 10.7 percent. These measures are good for showing projects results. The overall quality level will be impacted but not by a lot of change in sigma level.

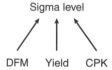

Sigma level

DFM   Yield   CPK

Introducing lean manufacturing with Six Sigma, eliminating waste, also becomes a major thrust. The possibility of activity indicators along with an outcome indicator comes into play. The activity possibilities are the number of processes reviewed, and value was made along with number of nonvalue activities eliminated.

The outcome measure is to reduce cost. In this case, cost of poor quality (COPQ) becomes our outcome metric (see Figure 1.7). If it is reduced significantly, our actions were successful.

If a corporate performance measure is insensitive to small improvements, look at lower-level measures that affect it. Choose one or more that is sensitive; that is, it shows improvement even if small. This makes the indicator actionable and sensitive and motivates both teams and management.

3.4.3.9 Method 9: Process Flowchart Method of Identifying Measures

Developing process metrics starts with flowcharting the process. The job process flowchart is an excellent one to use. Each activity is visited, one by one, and the questions are asked: "Do I need to measure this activity or the process at this point? What should I measure? Are the data available? What is to be measured on the vertical axis and on the horizontal axis?"

Put an M and number as you go through the process (M_1, M_2, M_3).

Sometimes a Q (Q_1, Q_2, Q_3) is used for a quality measure. The number of measures is not important, but the

Job flow chart

Who	Measure	Title	Target
M_1	M_1		
M_2	M_2		
M_3 Q_1	M_3		

impact or importance of the measure is. The measures should tell how well the process is working and highlight problem areas or potential problem areas. See Chapter 4 for examples of applying this method, including jump-starting a process to increase performance.

3.4.3.10 Method 10: Stages/phases Measurement

Often major improvement efforts are implemented and measures of progress and success are needed to keep management apprised. These efforts are implemented in stages or phases. They often involve communications, meetings, employee training, identification of problems, team formulation, and following a problem-solving process, leading after several stages/phases to some results. (For example, see a quality improvement initiative or Six Sigma.) The measures first start as those of progress. They include: how many employees have been trained, how many teams have been formed, what percentage of employees are involved, how many facilitators have been trained, and what is the ratio of teams to facilitators. Later, management looks for results, such as problems solved, savings or cost avoided, and indicators that were improved.

The metric development process for these types of measures are:

Beginning		Six months	Year
Phase 1	Phase 2	Phase 3	Phase 4
Measures of progress			Measures of results

Step 1. Write the objective of the effort.

Step 2. Envision the activities/events in implementing the effort. Who, when, why, where, and how questions should be asked, and jot down your ideas of implementation. Identify stages of development or phases in implementation, whichever is most appropriate.

Step 3. Identify the things, events, or activities that should be measured.

Step 4. Develop the indicators of progress.

Step 5. Identify the expected results.

Step 6. Determine how the results would be obtained and how they should be measured.

Step 7. Determine when each indicator should be employed by stages or phases and when one would be discontinued and others started.

Example:

Company ABC is planning to implement a continuous improvement program (CIP). Management wishes to have measures in place to know how the program is going. A team of promoters of continuous improvement was put together. The team was limited to eight people, each from a different functional area. The leadership council gave them:

Step 1. The objective is to implement continuous improvement philosophy throughout the company so that our processes can be improved to at least four sigma quality performance levels and our customer satisfaction index be no lower than outstanding by end of year 2008.

Step 2. Envision the activities/events necessary in implementing CIP.

The team met to accomplish Step 2. Before meeting, they had researched other companies' efforts that had been reported in ASQ and IIE magazines. The team leader had visited a company that was implementing a similar program. She took notes of their efforts, problems, and successes. She shared the notes with the rest of the team.

The team brainstormed a list of activities. They were:

1. Leaders give support speeches and introduction to CIP.

2. Training program needs to be developed.

3. Employees trained in concept.

4. Process improvement teams formed.

5. Statistical specialists will need to be identified and trained.

6. Teams will need to be trained in problem solving.

7. Key processes quality levels need to be estimated and prioritized as to the ones needing the most improvements.

8. Teams need to be assigned to the poor performing processes to improve them.

9. Problem-solving facilitators should be trained and assist each team in improving their processes.

10. Teams should meet regularly and stay the course until improvement results.

The team felt that these were the 10 items that needed to be done.

Step 3. Identify the things or activities that need to be measured. Green-lighting, or open discussion focused on the step, resulted in identifying these areas needing measuring at first.

Phase 1. Getting Started: First Year and a Half

- The percentage of employees trained in CIP

- The number of processes identified needing improvement

- The percentage of poorly performing processes that have a team assigned

- The percentage of teams that have a trained facilitator

- The percentage of statistical specialists trained and ready to assist teams

It is obvious that the items proposed for measurement are in actuality the things (objectives) we want to happen.

Phase 2. Problem Solving: 18 Months–Two Years

The team felt that in this stage there should be evident progress in the processes. They felt that a few of the other indicators should be kept, at least through this stage. The ones they felt should continue to be measured are:

Percentage of employees trained in concept	Target: 100 percent
Percentage of teams assigned to processes	Target: 70 percent
Needing improvement	80 percent
The new indicator needed is	100 percent
Percentage of teams formed that are in the analysis phase of the problem-solving process.	Target is 100% by end of year

At this time, the progress indicators are no longer needed. The shift is to achieving results. The team and management will need to readdress these measures over time since things change. Sometimes jump-starting a program (see Chapter 7) is needed to overcome stagnancy and get rapid improvement in an activity.

Phase 3. Results: Two Years to Four Years

The team realized that during this phase, all the other efforts should start materializing. Now is the time to start moving from measures of progress to measures of success. The team felt that a couple of progress indicators should be maintained along with result measures.

Progress measures	Results measures
• Percentage of active teams that have gone through the implementation step of the problem-solving process	• Percentage of key processes meeting five sigma quality levels
	• Amount of savings
• Percentage of key poor performing processes* that are being addressed	• Amount of cost avoidances

*Poor performing defined as not meeting five sigma quality levels.

The results measures will be kept in place until the expected quality levels are achieved. The progress measures will be measured until close to 100 percent is achieved.

The measures presented were selected by the team members. Of course, there were numerous other possibilities. Training and developing Green Belts, which are the number of Six Sigma Black Belts in the getting-started phase. Process measures and machine measures such as utilization, efficiency, yield, and productivity are only a few of the possibilities. The results stages, rework, and number of projects with savings greater than $250,000 are examples. The objectives of the phase and overall program dictate the right measures. Without the measures, no one would know the progress of implementation or whether the program was on a track to success or whether it resulted in a major success, in some success, or in failure.

3.4.3.11 Method 11: The POEM

Teams are formed when they have been assigned to solve a problem or to look for problems in a process.

Roses are red
Violets are blue.
Follow the POEM
If you want to improve.

P Is for Problem or Purpose

A team that does not have a problem should find a problem that when solved will either reduce cost, decrease delivery time, improve reliability or quality, enhance safety, and improve customer satisfaction. Often one solution affects more than one indicator or key result area.

O Is for Observe or Opportunity

The team can observe operations. For example, how do the employees serve the customers? Are there any long lines? What products are returned? How many angry or satisfied customers are there? What types of problems are experienced? What is the attitude and performance of employees interfacing with customers? There are numerous opportunities.

The team identifies the most important opportunity that needs the most improvement (see the Decision Grid).

Decision grid

	Works well	Needs a little improvement	Needs a lot of improvement
Very important			$\otimes$
Important			
Somewhat important			
Not important			

E Is for Evaluate

Once you have made your observations and selected your problem or opportunity, you will need to collect data. A check sheet will probably need to be developed to use in collecting data (see Chapter 6).

A flowchart of the process will help you understand the activities and determine where in the process to measure.

M Is for Measure

Identify the measure(s), check against "good metrics criteria," and develop the metrics package. Be sure to define what is to be measured, when, and by whom, and what is included and what is not. This is called an operational statement.

Determine which type of chart is best for the measure (normally a line graph or bar chart). Collect data and baseline the chart or graph. Set a realistic but stretch target. Graph the measure. If best-in-class data are available, plot them on the graph.

Maintain the graph at the recommended frequency. Keep it visible and check trends for improvement or no improvement.

3.4.3.11.1 AIM (Analyze, Improve, and Manage)

If the problem is not improving (the trend is not going in the right direction), analyze for root causes (fishbone diagram).

Select the most probable causes and verify with data whether they are root causes. Develop countermeasures that are feasible and effective. Sell them to appropriate people, boards, or committees. Develop and implement an improvement implementation plan. Monitor and manage the process to include control to be sure that it is stable and in statistical control and that the process capability is what is desired.

After POEM, AIM can lead to success and become a cornerstone for continuous improvement efforts.

3.4.3.11.2 Generate New Performance Indicators Summary

Ten methods using 14 or more tools/techniques were outlined and examples shown on pages 24 and 25. A summary of these methods follows. The best time to use the method is outlined and then the specific tools/techniques paramount to each method.

3.4.4 Indicator Evaluation

Once three to five performance indicators have been developed, a method to select one or two is needed. Applying this method also ensures that one fully understands the indicator and the message it sends to all employees.

An ideal indicator is one that meets most of the key characteristics of indicators (Tsao, 2000). It fails if it does not meet the four "Musts" criteria. The characteristics, the ones the author has found important and useful, with definitions, are:

Musts (If any receive a no, it fails the criteria.)

1. Measurable

   • Can be quantified by formula, ratio, index, ranking, and so forth.

2. Auditable and repeatable

   • Information is accurate, and a source document list, chart, or a computer screen is available.
   • Similar performance changes will produce similar results repeatedly.
   • Multiple observers of the indicator would agree on what is good performance and what is bad.

3. Customer oriented

   • Established with the customers' needs in mind, both external and internal customers. (Normally, an average does not measure well how customers' needs are being satisfied.)

4. Cost effectiveness

   • Benefits gained from a measure must exceed the costs associated with collecting the data.

Summary of methods: Techniques used

Method	Best use when?	Objectives	Brainstorming	NGT	Stratification	Process flowchart	Word association	SMART	Surveys	Research for traditional	CSFs	Envision the outcome	Factor analysis	Efficiency formulas
1. Title-to-title method	Simple measures. Measures items, events, activities that just in name or title implies chat should be measured.	X	X				X							
2. SMART objectives	When objectives are not specific. Put when and how much into objective.	X						X						
3. Index: A. Surveys	A. No data available, know the purpose or objective. Determine questions, scales, write question (Likert), administer, analyze, and present results in indicator form. Need to get periodically.	X												
B. Efficiency	B. Identify purpose; then use four deficiency types to determine one that meets your purpose.													X
4. Group dynamics development	When there are a lot of possible performance indicators (could be traditional indicators). Group knowledge is evident and group dynamics can produce several possible measures.	X	X	X						X				
5. Structure tree what – how chart	Know purpose, but not sure of all its components and possible measures.	X			X									
6. Project measures development – CSF – objectives – measures	Flowchart the activities needed to be done to accomplish the project. Identify the critical success factors, turn into objectives and then measures.	X				X		X			X			

Summary of methods: Techniques used (continued)

Method	Best use when?	Objectives	Brainstorming	NGT	Stratification	Process flowchart	Word association	SMART	Surveys	Research for traditional	CSFs	Envision the outcome	Factor analysis	Efficiency formulas
7. Meet desired outcomes	Have a desired outcome and need to figure out how to achieve it. Determine the factors that influence the outcome and then the activities to make the factors and outcome happen.												X	X
8. Assessing lower level measures as to impact to a higher level measure	When you have traditional indicators that are important but high level, you need to go to actionable indicators that support or impact them. Actionable? Yes_____ No_____	X			X				X					
9. Process flowchart method	Flowchart the process. At each activity or decision point, ask does a measure need to be accomplished?	X			X									
10. Stages/ phases measurement	Major programs/ initiatives are implemented. There is a need to track progress in the implementation.	X	X	X					X		X			
11. Follow the POEM then AIM for success	Team has a problem or purpose, little data but observation of a process or processes can provide data. A continuous improvement tool.	X			X									X

- In many cases, data for an indicator should be available from existing management information systems.
- Sometimes use of a scatter diagram will show that another measure that is cost effective to attain is highly correlated with one whose cost is prohibited.

Desired criteria (characteristics of good indicators)

1. Sends the right message

    - The objectives and message the indicator sends are consistent. The action the company, division, and department personnel take is based on the message about what the company desires.

2. Coverage

    - Adequate coverage of the mission, objectives, functions, and organizational achievements should be accomplished. If not, those being measured will focus on the indicators identified as important by their management, and other important areas could suffer.

3. Sensitive

    - Actual changes in performance are reflected accurately in the trends of the indicator. The degree to which an indicator can capture and portray changes accurately depends on whether the indicators and the objectives are correlated or sensitive.
    - Cause-and-effect relationship has been established.

4a. Believable and acceptable

    - The measures including the targets should be believable and acceptable by the majority of the department and company or team being measured.

4b. Understandable (simple)

    - The extent to which the relationship between the level of performance and the measure will be understood by the department, group, or individuals being measured. Make the indicators simple and understandable.

5. Useful (drives action) and controllable

    - To be useful, an indicator should drive/guide us toward some effective action. If the trend is not in the right direction, action needs to be taken. Indicators must be controlled by the ones being measured.

- Some of these can be combined if desired (believable and acceptable with average or understandable). Also, they can be varied, except the MUSTS, as the team or individual developing the indicators desired.

Let's look how easily these criteria can be used and how they help us select a good indicator. Let's revisit Method 5—Structure Tree and add the criteria as Step 2 (see Figure 3.6). Select the indicator.

Step 1. What to measure, ask how, and write down potential measures.

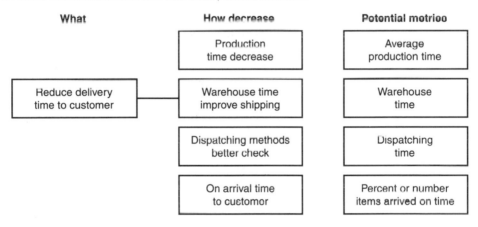

Step 2. Select the indicator – evaluating indicator as to its effectiveness.

Checks Characteristics of a good indicator	Production time	Warehouse time	Dispatching time	Percent or number times arrived on time
Measurable	⊙ 5	○ 3	○ 3	⊙ 5
Customer oriented	○ 3	○ 3	○ 3	⊙ 5
Sends right message	○ 3	○ 3	○ 3	⊙ 5
Data available/cost effective	⊙ 5	○ 3	⊙ 5	⊙ 5
Simple/understandable/believable	⊙ 5	⊙ 5	⊙ 5	⊙ 5
Sensistive/coverage	○ 3	○ 3	○ 3	⊙ 5
Congruent/useful/actionable	△ 1	△ 1	△ 1	⊙ 5
Auditable/repeatable	⊙ 5	⊙ 5	⊙ 5	⊙ 5
Total score	30	26	28	40

⊙ 5 points   ○ 3 points   △ 1 point

Figure 3.5   Method 5: Structure tree/What-how chart.   *(continued)*

Step 3. Graph. *(continued)*

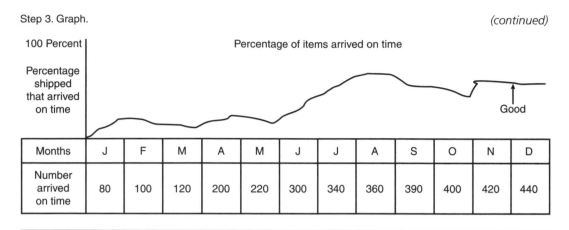

Months	J	F	M	A	M	J	J	A	S	O	N	D
Number arrived on time	80	100	120	200	220	300	340	360	390	400	420	440

Figure 3.5 Method 5: Structure tree/What-how chart.

3.4.5 Indicators Can Send the Wrong Message: Chicken Efficiency

Mark G. Brown (1996) states that a fast-food chain specializing in chicken has a favored measure. It is called "chicken efficiency." All the restaurant's personnel know that this is the key measure. Graphs showing chicken efficiency by month are developed and sent to the management.

$$\text{Chicken efficiency} = \frac{\text{X number of pieces sold}}{\text{Number thrown away}}$$

The number thrown away depends on the strict standards of how long the chicken can sit under the heat lights before it must be discarded.

What performance will chicken efficiency drive? Management had hoped it would drive efforts to sell chicken, because the more they sell, the less that remains to be thrown away. What it really drives is "Don't cook chicken; wait for customer and then cook the order. No chicken has to be thrown away." However, the customer has to wait for 20 minutes. Some will wait (they love the chicken and are patient), and others will leave.

Maximizing chicken efficiency causes customer dissatisfaction in that wait time is increased. It is common for manipulating an indicator that another important one may be negatively impacted.

No chicken is left over. However, customer satisfaction suffers because some customers leave because they don't want to wait. Those who stay are less happy than if they received their order upon arrival. Indicators can send a wrong message and therefore be counterproductive and hamper customer satisfaction. In developing and using a performance indicator, one has to be sure the people that impact the measures impact it in the manner desired.

4

Constructing the Indicator Graph and the Metric Package

4.1 OBJECTIVES

1. Understand all elements of a metric, commonly called the metrics package.

2. Learn how to select the right graph.

3. Become familiar with strategies for plotting the data.

4. Be able to select an excellent presentation format.

4.2 GLOSSARY

Air Force metric package—What constitutes a metric; operational definition and data collection plan, presentation format, and measurement.

graph strategy—Selection of a line graph, bar chart, column chart, pie chart, or some other graph.

operational definition—What should be collected and what should not.

plotting strategy—Decision on how to compute the data for graphing—for example, 12 month's average, annualized, 12 month's ending, percent, or numbers.

presentation format—How data are displayed: on the computer, posted in a visible place, and so forth.

4.3 AIR FORCE METRIC PACKAGE

The Air Force's metric package consists of three basic elements: the operational definition, the actual measurement and recording of data, and the metric presentation. Together, these three are called the metric package (see Figure 4.1).

The metric package is an excellent way to look at a metric. It is more than just a chart.

4.4 OPERATIONAL DEFINITION

"Operational Definition is the precise definition explanation of the process being measured. It is who, what, why, when, where and how of the metric. The measurement and data collection is the translation of data from the process into

---

7 Step Metric Development Process

1. Identify purpose and establish objectives. (Chapter 3)
2. Determine if existing traditional indicators are available and are appropriate. (Chapter 3)
3. Generate new possible performance indicators. (Chapter 3)
4. Evaluate indicators for effectiveness. (Chapter 3)
5. **Construct indicator graphs. (Chapter 4)**
6. Select targets and plot on graph. (Chapter 5)
7. Monitor and act. (Chapter 6)

• Internal understanding

• Process signal

External communication

```
Operational
definition
      |
      v
Measurement
      |
      v
Presentation
```

• Enough detail to make sure it is repeatable and hard to manipulate

• Chart selection
• Get data
• Baseline data
• Plotting strategy

Metric formula, graph, responsible person, data collection information

Figure 4.1 Metric package.

understandable and useful information. The metric presentation is the metric's communication link to the process customer and process manager" (Sink and Tuttle, 1989).

Data should be collected in sufficient amounts at the beginning to have at least six months to a year of past data to plot as a baseline to compare future results against. This action is called baselining the graph.

4.5 CONSTRUCTING THE GRAPH

4.5.1 Selecting the Best Chart

There are basically only five quantitative charts to select from. There are several other nonquantitative charts, such as maps, flowcharts, matrices, organization charts, and PDPC (program decision program charts). The latter are useful in many other endeavors, such as planning, but not for displaying a metric/performance indicator.

Of course, the charts shown in Figure 4.2 can be altered in numerous ways, such as stacking the bar charts, combining a bar chart and line chart, and using different color codes or double lines. They can be used in combination with column

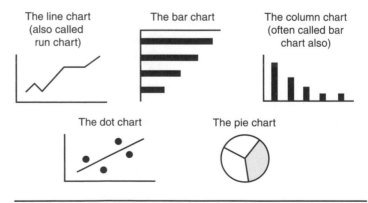

Figure 4.2 Charts.

charts and line charts. We use a process to start with the data and end up with a chart (Zelazny, 1991).

Step 1. Determine your specific point (objective or message).

Charts have measures (dollars, utilization, productivity, and so on). These measures don't determine the appropriate chart; the point or message that you wish to convey does. Sketch several charts using the data. It will become apparent which chart best highlights your message. A particular chart may have several possible messages, and you must pick the one you wish to emphasize (see Figure 4.3).

These messages are helpful in explaining the graph. The primary message is reduce the errors. Having fewer errors is good.

Step 2. Identify the comparison that needs to be made to get the point or message across.

Zelazny shows five types of comparisons are possible (see Figure 4.4).

Step 3. Select the best chart form.

The message will always imply one of the five comparisons. The comparisons lead to one of the five quantitative charts (Zelazny, 1991).

For component comparisons, the pie chart is the best. It is very popular but is not as useful for other comparisons as the other charts. When item comparisons are made, the bar chart is used. For time series, two charts, the column chart and the line graph, are commonly used and sometimes

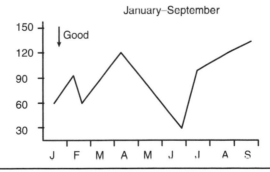

Figure 4.3   Number of errors.

Type component	Percent of a total	In June, the sales increase represents 30 percent of the total increase this year
Item comparison	Ranking of item	Lightning caused twice as many interruptions as cable failures
Time series	Change over time	Interest rates have steadily dropped over the last six months
Frequency distribution comparison	Items within ranges	Our product is normally delivered in 5 to 6 working days
Correlation comparison	Relationship between variables	Mortgage amounts increase with buyer's annual income

Figure 4.4 Comparisons.

together. In key performance indicators, they together make up 95 percent of the charts used. When other charts are used, they are shown by different periods. This is because you are comparing results over a time period. The frequency distribution chart is the column chart. For correlation comparison, the dot chart is predominant. However, using two bar charts (when only two items are correlated) side by side is useful.

Most indicators will use a topic title. The title of the measure is on the Y axis of a line chart.

For presentations or analysis, the title can be the message, such as "Northern Division accounted for 40 percent of the sales increase." This way your audience gets the point right away. In performance indicators, the title sends a message. The ones affected will want to improve it, especially if the chart has a target. The performance indicator must send the right message. Once an Air Force wing staff was developing its corporate indicators. One of the suggested performance indicators was to reduce the findings of their environmental self-audits. Before the final selection was made, the staff members realized that this was not appropriate, because the reason they do the audit is to reduce the Environmental Protection Agency's findings, which lead to dollar fines. The self-audit indicator would have sent the wrong message.

Spider charts show several indicators' present level of performance on one chart. The spider chart is constructed by first drawing a circle. Next, draw from the center (proportionally) the number of lines for which you have objectives or measures. Then scale the lines (using appropriate scales depending on the units of measure). Next, plot the present values for each measure. The outside circle is 100 percent. Starting at the centers, connect the dots (see Figure 4.5).

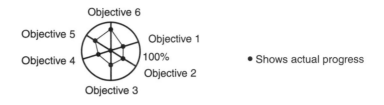

Figure 4.5   Spider chart.

Column chart (sometimes called a bar chart)

1. Place on the X axis (horizontal axis) the items or things being compared.

2. On the Y axis (vertical axis) show the quantities (that is, frequency of events in different locations or cost of different types of interruptions).

3. Draw vertical bars (spacing is up to you, depending only on your preference) of uniform width equal to the quantity or frequency of the item. For horizontal bars, reverse the contents of the axis.

Let's graph the number of interruptions by days (Monday through Friday). See Figure 4.6.

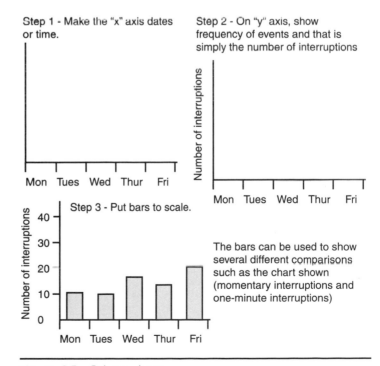

Figure 4.6   Column charts.

Days	M	T	W	T	F
Number of interruptions	10	8	14	12	18

Step 1. The days, Monday through Friday, are being compared, so they go on the X axis.

Step 2. On the Y axis, show the frequency of events, which is simply the number of interruptions.

Step 3. Draw the vertical bars (same width) up to the number of interruptions. For example, on Monday 10 interruptions occurred (bar goes up to 10 vertical scale).

Column charts are primarily used for comparisons. Sometimes trend lines can be shown in a bar graph. However, line graphs are the most common graphs for depicting trends.

Line Graphs

Line graphs are used most commonly for indicators. They show trend lines, which are so important for showing success (improvement) or problems. For simplicity and feasibility, to quickly gauge how things are going, a "good arrow" showing which direction is favorable is placed on the graph (bar graphs too). At the bottom, it is good to show a legend or key (for each line, if more than one is on the graph). To distinguish between lines, colors or different dot-dash combinations are used. It is good to show at the bottom of the graph the data source and who is responsible for updating the graph. The title of the graph should include some of the words used on the Y axis or at least be congruent. The X axis normally is time (days, months, years). Show the graph strategy (12 months ending, monthly, 12-month average, daily)

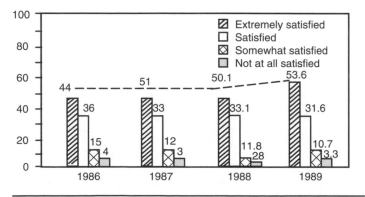

Figure 4.7 Residential customers' overall satisfaction (fourth quarter).

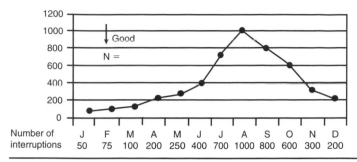

Number of interruptions	J	F	M	A	M	J	J	A	S	O	N	D
	50	75	100	200	250	400	700	1000	800	600	300	200

Figure 4.8 Number of electrical service primary interruptions (1990).

under the title (see Figure 4.7). Dotted lines show projections or targets. The darkest line shows the most recent performance.

Construction of a line graph (see Figure 4.8)

Step 1. Show intervals on the horizontal axis (usually time).

Step 2. Show quantities on the vertical axis (frequency of events).

Step 3. Plot the data and draw a trend line to connect the quantities observed on each successive item.

Let's plot the number of electrical service interruptions by month. The graph shows that the number of interruptions peak in August.

Construction of Pie Chart

Step 1. Calculate the size of each wedge by taking the value of each item and dividing it by the total value of all items.

Step 2. Multiply by 360 to determine the number of degrees for each wedge. Use a protractor to plot the degrees accurately.

Step 3. Divide the pie (circle) into wedges so that each represents the desired proportional part of the whole.

The total service unavailability in 2001 and 2002 was composed of the following:

	Environmental	Accidents	Equipment factor	Unknown interruptions
2001	50	15	25	10
2002	30	15	45	10

Construct a 2001 pie chart and a 2002 pie chart. (See Figure 4.9)

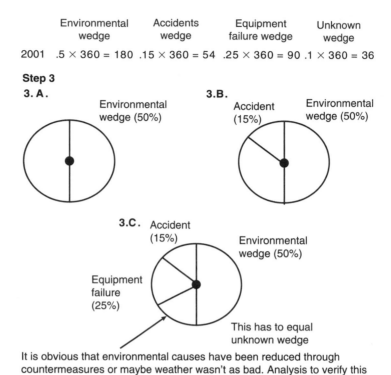

	Environmental wedge	Accidents wedge	Equipment failure wedge	Unknown wedge
2001	.5 × 360 = 180	.15 × 360 = 54	.25 × 360 = 90	.1 × 360 = 36

Step 3

3.A.

Environmental wedge (50%)

3.B.

Accident (15%)   Environmental wedge (50%)

3.C. Accident (15%)

Environmental wedge (50%)

Equipment failure (25%)

This has to equal unknown wedge

It is obvious that environmental causes have been reduced through countermeasures or maybe weather wasn't as bad. Analysis to verify this is needed. The large change (increase) in equipment failure needs to be investigated to determine causes so that corrective actions can be taken.

Figure 4.9 Pie chart.

For the majority of indicators measuring problem areas or objectives, the vertical axis is normally what you are measuring (number of or percentage of something) and the X axis is time (days, weeks, months, or years). Normally, the trend is what you are looking for (up, down, or getting better or worse). Therefore, a line graph would be the most appropriate graph to use.

An exception on good arrows:

Sometimes one direction is not right. An example is when a range is good, having both a lower and upper desired control limit (see Figure 4.10).

Moving averages

A moving average is a smoothing technique to be considered whenever particular data has wide fluctuations (15 percent or more variation) from period to period. Results from a fixed number of periods are averaged by dropping the "oldest" and figuring the average again using the newest

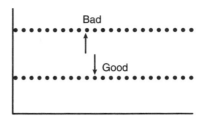

Figure 4.10 Action limits.

data point. For example, if the service unavailability for a utility for each month were:

Calculate for January 31, 1991

1990   1991

Jan	Feb	Mar	Apr	May	Jun	Jul	Aug	Sep	Oct	Nov	Dec	Jan
2.0	5.0	5.5	2.5	7.0	6.5	10	12	4	5	8	?	1.5

The 12-month ending number would be calculated by dropping the 2.0 for January 1990 and adding the 1.5 for January 1991.

For beginning of February 1990 to January 1991:

$$\frac{5.0+5.5+2.5+7.0+6.5++10+12+4+5+8+2+1.5}{12} = \frac{69}{12} = 5.75$$

For 1990: $\dfrac{2+5+5.5+2.5+7+6.5+10+12+4+5+8+2}{12} = \dfrac{69.5}{12} = 5.79$

The January 1991 12 MOE (month ending) is 5.75 compared to 5.79 for 1990 12 MOE. The reduction is due to the better performance in January 1991 compared to January 1990.

Percentage versus numbers

Using charts that show numbers is excellent, especially for analysis purposes. Percentages are good for management information. Often it is useful to use both numbers and percentages (see Figure 4.11).

%   N = Number of observations

Figure 4.11 Number of objectives.

Existing Indicators

Before generating new indicators, review the indicators presently being used or used in the past. Interviewing key personnel to assess the value of existing indicators may prove helpful. Also, review databases to determine what kind of information is readily available.

4.6 DATA COLLECTION

Once the operational definition is developed for the performance indicator, a data collection plan should be developed. The data collection plan should tell what is to be collected, when (frequency) it needs to be collected, by whom (who is responsible), the reason or objective for collecting the data, and the source of the data. Before data collection, it is absolutely essential to make sure the cost of collecting the data is worth the effort. In other words, the importance of the measure must outweigh the cost of data collection.

Data should be collected to include a year or at least six months (if possible) so the chart or graph can have this data plotted. It provides a baseline of past performance. A comparison of present to the same period last year is normally interesting and helpful. It enables calculations of important features such as labor productivity.

$$\text{Labor productivity} = \frac{\dfrac{\text{Earned hours}}{\text{Total hours}}}{\dfrac{\text{Earned hours baseline}}{\text{Total hours baseline}}}$$

The source of the data can be a management information system, manual tabulation from records, check sheets, observations, or another source. It is helpful to write the source on the graph presentation so it is visible to anyone using the performance indicator.

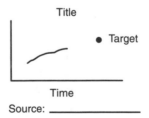

The operational definition tells us exactly what needs to be collected. From when to when is important. State what is included or excluded, such as the graph doesn't include weekend measurements or uncommon events such as tornados or hurricanes. Without tying this down, comparisons between departments or industry cannot be useful. It is not unusual that different organizations include different information on the same traditional indicators.

The best-in-class performance should be annotated to show what's possible. Again let's review what a metric is:

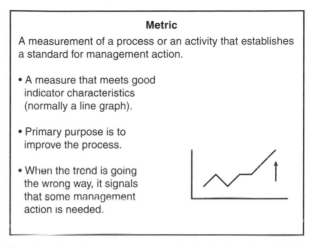

Metric

A measurement of a process or an activity that establishes a standard for management action.

• A measure that meets good indicator characteristics (normally a line graph).

• Primary purpose is to improve the process.

• When the trend is going the wrong way, it signals that some management action is needed.

The basic format recommended by the Malcolm Baldrige National Quality Award appears in Figure 4.12.

4.7 GRAPH STRATEGY

Now we know the types of charts, what we are going to collect, and when we will collect it. The next matter is to construct the graph. The indicator, what we are measuring, goes on the Y axis, and time (normally in months) goes on the X axis. The subject or topic goes up high in the middle. The target is shown as a point, and the line from the present to the target is a dotted line. Best-in-class performance is shown if known (see Figure 4.12). The formula, data collection, process owner, and other pertinent information is shown below the X axis on the right side of the chart. A "good" arrow shows whether the preferred trend goes up or down. When percentages are used, the total number is shown as N = _____ in the upper left corner.

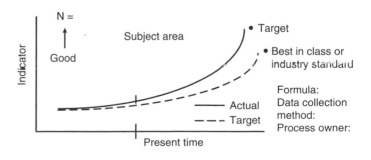

Figure 4.12   Metric presentation.

PLOTTING STRATEGY

1. Numbers	Analysis, system of indicators.
2. Cumulative line	Trends desired and commonly used in conjunction with numbers.
3. Annualized	Enables a person to take a montly figure and estimate it's impact over a year.
4. Standardized	Have a denominator in the indicator. Standardization enables everything to be compared on an equal basis.
5. 12 months average	Monthly or yearly targets not important. Seasonality not evident. Used often in establishing a baseline year.
6. 12 months ending	A yearly target is important and the indicator is tracked at least monthly.
7. Year to date	When it is important how we are doing from January to now.
8. Percent	Large numbers—high level outcome monitoring. Shown (number of data points) also in the graph.
9. High-level index	Stay away from unless no other approach is feasible. They give trends that are not good for analysis or to show how you got to where you are.
10. Ranking	Ranking from 0 to 10 based on some criteria—okay if no other measurements exist.

1. Numbers	Numbers plotted by time.
2. Cumulative line	Plot first month, plot second month's figure and first months figure ... plot last months figure plus all preceding ones.
3. Annualized	Multiply monthly figure by 12 to represent for a year what the month would look like for a year.
4. Standardized	Take number of interruptions for a district and divide by miles of line—makes the figures comparable (division to division, district to district). The denominator enables comparison to be made.

Dec 31, 1988 12 months ending is 212
For Jan 1989, the number is 12

District A

$$\frac{5000 \text{ interruptions}}{18,000 \text{ miles of line}} = .278$$

District B

$$\frac{6000 \text{ interruptions}}{20,000 \text{ miles of line}} = .3$$

January 12 month ending—drop January 1988 10
add January 1989 12 214

5. 12 months average—December 31, 1988

$$\frac{212}{12} = 17.67$$

6. 12 months ending

Jan	Feb	Mar	Apr	May	Jun	Jul	Aug	Sep	Oct	Nov	Dec
10	14	21	18	11	16	21	32	18	12	19	20

Each month—add and drop the figure for the month, last year—add all months and divide by 12.

Figure 4.13   Plotting strategy.   *(continued)*

(continued)

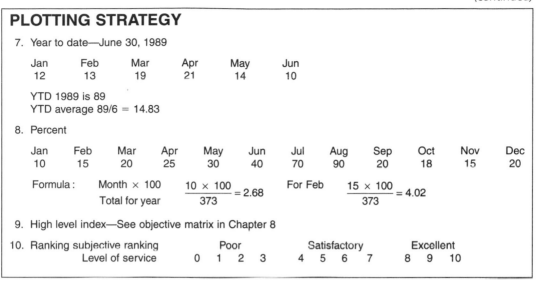

Figure 4.13 Plotting strategy.

4.8 PLOTTING STRATEGY

Graphs when shown over time (time is X axis) become performance indicators. The strategy in plotting the indicator begins first in determining the unit (pounds, interruptions, percentages, errors) for the Y axis. Next, determine the time period on the X axis.

Ten of the most common graph strategy types are shown in Figure 4.13, along with when to use them.

4.9 PRESENTATION FORMAT

Presentation format consists of the graph (chart selected) plotted showing baseline data (one year or more data if available) and projected target(s), who collected the data and where, and the formula.

The presentation should be made visible in a computer system or posted on a bulletin board or white board so involved employees have ready access.

5

Set Targets

5.1 OBJECTIVES

1. Learn process or procedure for setting targets for performance measures/metrics.

2. Be able to select the best method for your performance measures/targets.

3. Learn how to use (Steps 1–6 of the metric development process) by reviewing two team examples of developing corporate performance indicators.

5.2 GLOSSARY

methods—Eight methods are outlined for setting targets. Any one of them may be appropriate for you.

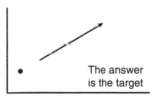

Where do you want to go and
how long do you want to take?

The answer
is the target

You are here

target—A goal or level of performance you wish to reach.

5.3 WHAT IS A TARGET?

A target is a goal or level of performance you wish to reach. It is a goal or objective used to measure performance and usually is expressed as a numerical value or percentage. Once you decide what performance level you need to reach, you can compare that with the current situation. If there is a significant difference (gap), then this may be your long-range (three to five years) target (close the gap). Next, strategies,

7 Step Metric Development Process
1. Identify purpose and establish objectives. (Chapter 3)
2. Determine if existing traditional indicators are available and are appropriate. (Chapter 3)
3. Generate new possible performance indicators. (Chapter 3)
4. Evaluate indicators for effectiveness. (Chapter 3)
5. Construct indicator graphs. (Chapter 4)
6. Select targets and plot on graph. (Chapter 5)
7. Monitor and act. (Chapter 6)

Target	
What	Precise
How much	Quantity
When	Time frame

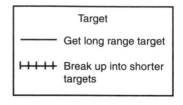

projects, and special circumstances should be analyzed to establish short-term targets (monthly and yearly).

Targets should be established using data, performing analysis, considering customer needs (internal or external customers), and establishing realistic but stretch targets. To ensure that targets are possible to achieve, projects should be identified and their contribution toward meeting the targets estimated. There should be sufficient contribution identified to meet each short-range target.

5.4 PROCEDURE FOR SETTING TARGETS

Targets are set after your indicator is selected and your chart type is identified and ready to be constructed.

Procedure for setting targets
1. Get data.
2. Analyze.
3. Establish number of percentage improvement for long range.
4. Establish time frames.
5. Determine method of distributing targets in short term.

5.5 TARGET METHODOLOGY

Eight methods can be used in setting or establishing targets. Also, some can be altered and some used as combinations, magnifying the number of methods possible.

Target methodology
• Benchmarking
• Performance/delivery targets
• American or Yankee spirit
• Trend line projection
• Back to the best
• Action limits
• Reduce range, variance, or standard deviation
• Management decree

5.5.1 Benchmarking

Benchmarking can be accomplished by comparing one of your processes with a process used by a competitor, similar organization, or an organization that does the same type of function. For example, most companies do billing. You do not have to compare your company against a company that makes the same products or services you do. Most companies do billing and also other support activities such as drafting, complaint management, or warehousing.

Figure 5.1 shows a six-step process. There are several different step processes, but all should lead to the same result (Camp, 1989, 1994).

Benchmarking enables an organization to find out what a best-in-class or world-class performance level is for a specific performance measure (see Figure 5.2).

An excellent strategic initiative is to go from present to best in class or higher or to even world-class target.

Business can use this method to transform their organizations into a top performer. The best way to get to the target is to use the technique of setting a target three to five years out and then allocating the contribution by year that adds to the total needed.

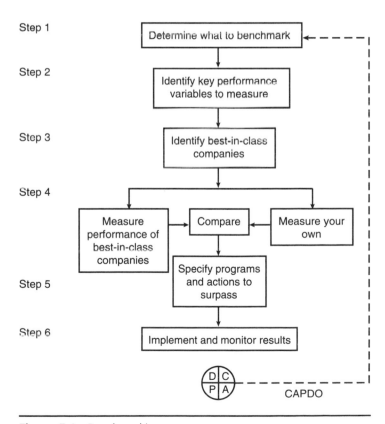

Figure 5.1 Benchmarking

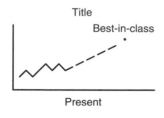

Figure 5.2   Best-in-class.

The primary failures of benchmarking are:

1. The team makes their visit prior to developing a benchmarking plan to include process flowchart, process metric to be benchmark identified, target desired, and so on. Without the plan, the trip is just a tour and results in no gain in performance.

2. Team tries to benchmark items that are not a process, such as organizational structure or roles and responsibilities.

3. Competitors do not like to give out information because it may jeopardize their market share. There are benchmarking warehouses or organizations that may prove helpful.

The main goal in target setting is to achieve a stretch target, one that can be achieved with countermeasures in a reasonable period.

5.5.2 Performance/Delivery Targets

In organizations that have several plants, service centers, or regional offices, setting performance and delivery targets is very useful. For the metric for which you are establishing a target, determine its level at each of the sites. Determine what makes the best performer achieve its level of performance. Do the same for the lowest, asking why it is the lowest performer. Using the data, determine how you can improve and set a target that would significantly improve the organization's overall performance.

Performance/delivery targets
1. Gather data and prepare histogram for system.
2. If you have several plants, shops, divisions, or regions, prepare a histogram for each.
3. Identify the best and worst performers. Determine what makes the best performers good and the worst performers bad. Can you improve the worst performers?
4. Using the data, develop a stretch target and then one for each division and plant.

5.5.3 American or Yankee Spirit

Dr. Noriaki Kano, a JUSE counselor, stated that if you don't know how far out to set a stretch target, use your Yankee spirit and set it for 50 percent over three to five years (see Figure 5.3). This is definitely a stretch; then, of course, figure out how you are going to achieve it.

• Long range target setting
• Breakthrough thinking
• Don't have any good rationale, but want significant improvement

50% improvement over three to five years

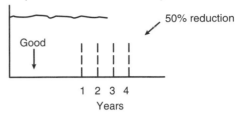

Figure 5.3   American or Yankee spirit.

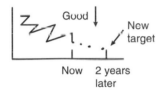

Figure 5.4   Trend line projection.

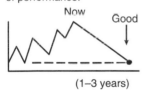

Figure 5.5   Back to the best.

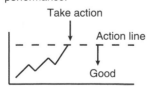

Figure 5.6   Action limits.

Although this method calls for 50 percent reduction, a greater or lesser percentage could be selected by management. It should be a stretch target, but also an achievable one. This method also applies to increased objectives such as growth.

5.5.4 Trend Line Projection

If the trend of the metric is moving in the right direction, then project it through three to five years and select that amount as your target (see Figure 5.4).

5.5.5 Back to the Best

Often, after baselining a metric, we discover that we had once been at the level we desire now. This becomes an easy-sell target: "We have done it before; why can't we do it again?" (See Figure 5.5.)

5.5.6 Action Limits

Targets have been often set with action limits in the past. Management, using its experience, sets an action limit that if exceeded requires immediate action (see Figure 5.6). This action could be projects, training, or other countermeasures to get the indicator back into acceptable levels of performance.

5.5.7 Reduce Range, Variance, or Standard Deviation

Calculate range, variance, and standard deviation for each service center, warehouse, regional office, and so forth for which you are setting targets. Then select a stretch amount to reduce the variability (see Figure 5.7).

Often the histogram shows excessively long times in one area and not in the other. Calculate what the parameter would be if these were eliminated. The target should be at least this amount.

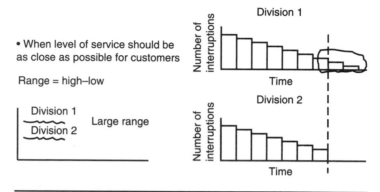

Figure 5.7 Reduce range, variance, or standard deviation.

5.6 A TEAM EXAMPLE

5.5.8 Management Decree

Management often sets targets based on experience or desires. If the target is reasonable, even though a stretch, the employees will embrace the target and do their best to achieve it. If not, it could become a laughable matter and little progress may be made even though the management emphasis may be high.

To really make maximum effort, employees must believe there is a chance of achieving the target. Management must provide adequate support to enable them to do so.

> Management decree often appears as if someone threw a dart at a dartboard and selected the number where it landed. Management must be ready to explain why the target was selected and why it is important to the organization.

5.6.1 Case 1: An Example of Metrics Development

A hypothetical team was formed with five middle management employees from different functional groups. They were championed by a vice president (in name only; he had retired on the job years earlier).

5.6.2 Team Objectives

The team objective was to design a new management system that satisfied both top management and the other employees. The team decided to research other systems such as total quality management, management by objectives, Malcolm Baldrige National Quality Award criteria, Six Sigma, continuous improvement, and any other approaches that have had some success. They identified several key areas in which to focus their research.

Leadership, processes, employee satisfaction, training, meetings, communication, measurement, and customer focus appeared to be important in all the systems that were studied.

5.6.3 Top Management

- Interviews

- Employee focus groups

- Customer panels

The team set up interviews with top and middle management. Also, they formed employee focus groups and established a few customer panels. Their findings were startling.

Management did not want to be involved. They wanted others to figure out what to do and then "just do it." Results, that's what's important. "Don't bother me with a bunch of fancy terms, especially statistical crap that no one really understands." The team decided that their new system shouldn't involve their management even though others had told them that management commitment was the foremost key to achieving success. Remembering that their objective was to satisfy everyone, they felt they must limit management's involvement or management would not be satisfied.

5.6.4 Employees

Employee focus groups led to other surprising findings. The majority stated that the best management system is to "just leave me alone and let me do my job." Meetings and learning about new "stuff" that's not helpful by sitting in classrooms talking about a bunch of theoretical stuff just doesn't make sense. We know our jobs. "Don't give us that accountability crap. Management is not held accountable to anything, why should we be?" Measurement of our processes and work takes time away from us doing the job. If you want us to meet a target, tell us and we will figure some way to do it.

Most of the team members understood that thinking because they felt that way before being selected to this team.

5.6.5 Communications

The team found out that the grapevine was extremely effective. No additional communications seemed necessary. If you want the "word to get out," just let anyone overhear something that they are not normally involved in and you can bet the word will spread like wildfire.

The team summarizes their findings from employees:

- No meetings.

- Leave communications alone.

- No new training.

- No new terminology and new processes.

- Don't hold employees accountable unless you (management) do the same.

- No measurements—they waste our time.

- "Leave us alone and we will get the job done" was the prevailing attitude.

5.6.6 Customers

Next, the team turned to the customer's focus. "The customer is always right" and "If we didn't have customers, we would not have a job" were some of the key phrases the team had heard on a benchmarking trip to a company that had received a few quality awards. However, the team noticed the employees sounded tired and overworked, but they couldn't put a finger on why.

Two customer panels (a group of selected customers who meet periodically to evaluate existing products or ideas for future product or service needs) were formed, and the team interviewed the customers. Much to their surprise, the customers seemed to be complaining.

The products did not seem to meet all their needs. The team checked, and the products did meet specifications.

The members thought, the customer got what we said they would get. Why are they complaining? If they don't like it, buy from someone else. What possible additional things would they desire? I wonder, if we built that, would they still complain? The team checked with management and asked why the company does not measure customer satisfaction. Management says some customers do give us some feedback. Others just complain about everything. So we don't need all these problems and complaints. They are the customer's fault in the first place.

The team did find the customer panels interesting but tiring; complaints are had to listen to for long periods. In future, the team decided the company should continue to have some customer panels so that it is obvious to the customers that they are one of our key focuses.

5.6.7 Developing the System

Name

Now the team was ready to design the new system. One of the active and vocal team members suggested that the new system needed a name. You can't sell a new system to top management without a catchy name or phrase. The team brainstormed a list of titles, discussed each, and multivoted down to three. Organizational excellence, company focus on happiness, and total satisfaction were the three finalists. Each had merit.

Organizational excellence is very good in that America seems to be in love with or in awe of the word *excellence*. A typical conception is "we don't know exactly what it is, but we will know it when we achieve it."

Company focus on happiness sounds good and sends a clear message, but maybe we should be sending other messages along with happiness, such as profit, people, and improvement.

Total satisfaction seems to capture our objective. Jim, a team member, jumped up and drew a diagram on the white board. It looked like this.

Everybody agreed that total satisfaction captured their intent. It has all the key players, including the customers.

5.6.8 Features

Now that we have the title (name), the team leader announced, we must set forth the features or principles of our new management system. The team openly discussed their findings from the interviews, focus groups, customer panels, and benchmarking trips. From the discussion, a motto seemed to come jumping out: "We plan to satisfy." Next, a list of characteristics was developed. They look like this:

Desired new management system

Desired features or Desired principles

1. Top management does not have to be involved or committed.

2. No systematic process needs to be followed to attain results.

3. Employees are not held accountable for their actions.

4. Managers and employees do not have to be bothered with a lot of new "stuff" that takes them away from their normal duties.

5. No additional training costs.

6. No meetings are necessary.

7. Increased communications not necessary since we have no progress on a journey to report.

8. Customers get what we manufacture. They like it or not like it. It's their choice but we will continue to focus on our customers.

9. Change—essentially a cultural change—is counterproductive.

10. Total satisfaction is our goal.

The team was thrilled. The 10 features would be their company's 10 commandments. They would represent the guiding light, moving the company to "total satisfaction." The team felt good about their recommendations. They developed a force field analysis to help sell them (see Figure 5.8).

The items pushing for in the force field analysis seem to overcome the ones pushing against. The team was now ready to present.

5.6.9 Team Presentation to Management

The team developed a few PowerPoint slides showing their objective, what they did to meet objectives, how they selected

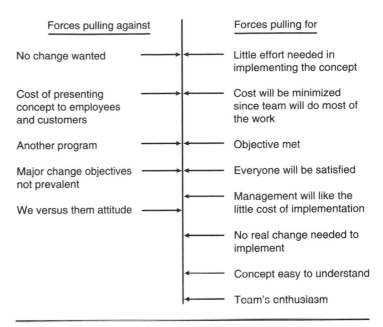

Figure 5.8 Force field analysis.

the name for the new management system, their motto, the characteristics of the new management system, and the force field analysis. The slides looked impressive. The team leader who was bucking for a promotion volunteered himself to present.

The leadership council (budget and financial planning) put the team's presentation on its agenda. The entire team was invited to attend.

As the team arrived, they were excited. The team leader made the presentation. The council members listened attentively. At the end, the council leader thanked the team for their fine efforts. He liked the name "total satisfaction." "That's what we need around here," he said. "I am sick of hearing complaints. Let's all get together and achieve total satisfaction." He went around the table and asked each leadership council member what they thought and whether they had any questions. Most of the members were very happy because the concept represents a "motherhood" objective and would require little or no effort on their part. One member did ask them about implementation. What has to be done and by whom? The team thought and answered happily that nothing has to be changed. All that has to be done is instilling the concept of working together to achieve total satisfaction. The council was pleased. They approved the concept and asked that the team come back next meeting with how they were going to measure the program's success. Everyone agreed this was an excellent idea.

5.6.10 Measurement

The team met the next day and first talked about the leadership council meeting. They were pleased the council had approved their concept and had congratulated them on their efforts. Then they got down to business. What do we measure? They decided on taking each major element or topic and determining what the indicator would be and whether the data were available already.

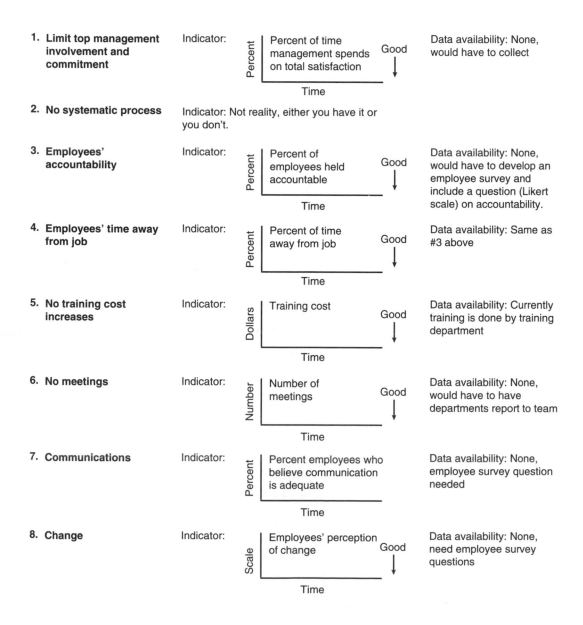

1. **Limit top management involvement and commitment**

   Indicator: Percent of time management spends on total satisfaction — Percent / Time — Good ↓

   Data availability: None, would have to collect

2. **No systematic process**

   Indicator: Not reality, either you have it or you don't.

3. **Employees' accountability**

   Indicator: Percent of employees held accountable — Percent / Time — Good ↓

   Data availability: None, would have to develop an employee survey and include a question (Likert scale) on accountability.

4. **Employees' time away from job**

   Indicator: Percent of time away from job — Percent / Time — Good ↓

   Data availability: Same as #3 above

5. **No training cost increases**

   Indicator: Training cost — Dollars / Time — Good ↓

   Data availability: Currently training is done by training department

6. **No meetings**

   Indicator: Number of meetings — Number / Time — Good ↓

   Data availability: None, would have to have departments report to team

7. **Communications**

   Indicator: Percent employees who believe communication is adequate — Percent / Time — Good ↓

   Data availability: None, employee survey question needed

8. **Change**

   Indicator: Employees' perception of change — Scale / Time — Good ↓

   Data availability: None, need employee survey questions

9. **Customer focus**

Indicator:

Percent | Customer satisfaction | Good
Time

Data availability: None, a survey would have to be developed and administered to customers. May cost a lot.

10. **Total satisfaction**

Indicator: #9 above plus percent employees' satisfied

Percent | Employees' satisfaction | Good
Time

Data availability: None, could be collected in numerous ways. Team will discuss and select method.

5.6.11 Measurement Summary

Data were not available on nine of the 10 proposed indicators. The cost of setting up data collection for these nine indicators would be substantial. Also, this would not be in accordance with the characteristics/principles. Especially, the employee survey violated the principle of leaving the employees alone. The team was concerned. They had a meeting in a few days to present how they were going to measure success. The meeting was adjourned and a new one set up the day before the leadership meeting. On this day, the team concluded that the whole purpose of their efforts is to reach total satisfaction. This is the first step in developing metrics. Employee satisfaction could be measured simply by having a box at the entrance door of each company facility and plates full of white and red poker chips. If the employees were satisfied, they should put a white chip in the box. (Management would also vote.) If not, they should select a red chip. Each employee was allowed to vote only once. At one hour after the company's regular starting hour had passed, a team member would pick up the box and take it to a conference room. The team would then count them and develop a percentage (white chips divided by total number of chips times 100). They developed a target or goal that at least 75 percent of all employees (top management, middle managers, workers) were satisfied. The team felt they had the answer. This is also a traditional indicator, thereby enabling the team to compare with other companies later. They were elated. They had already done Step 3, generate new indicators, and had rejected them due to cost of collecting the data. The total satisfaction measure met all of the good indicators' characteristics. It especially sends the right message, and it is economical.

On the next day, they presented their measurement plan. The council liked it. It was simple, inexpensive, and measured their objective of total satisfaction. They asked the team to measure the customers at the customers' panels by

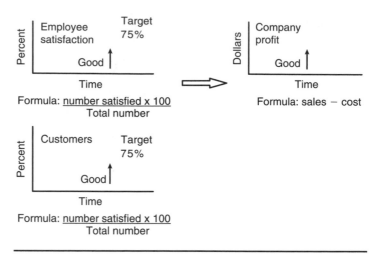

Figure 5.9   Total satisfaction.

using the same method. Of course, the team agreed. One of the council members sketched on a pad what appears in Figure 5.9.

This sketch became the cornerstone of the total satisfaction concept. It also showed Steps 5 and 6 of the metric development concept by constructing the indicators and setting targets. The monitoring and act step will be done in the future.

Evaluation:

This example is fictitious, of course. However, the author has encountered on numerous occasions, both in government and private industry, all of these views at one time or another. It would be nice if an effective management system could be developed using these principles. You would find more companies using it than Six Sigma, teams concept, or continuous improvement. However, this is impossible, and the idea of "no pain, no gain" certainly applies.

The measurement process is flawed in that the concept being measured does not include any possible process(es) improvements, no improved methods, no new employee problem-solving tools and techniques, and no leadership direction and commitment to a righteous purpose or vision. Any increases in profit could not be traced back to this concept and would be a result of some other company initiative. These measurements, by themselves, do not drive appropriate action (not actionable). Even if both customer panel and employee satisfaction measures reach 100 percent, they will most probably have little effect on profit (the bottom line). Using these principles, the company will probably be out of business in a few years, especially if their competition focuses on meeting customers' needs, measures its performance, continuously improves its processes, develops its

Measurement
• It does not happen all at once. There is no instant pudding.
• Change the rule and you will get a new number.
• Wherever there is fear, you will get wrong numbers.
• Does experience help? No! Not if we are doing the wrong thing.
Dr. W. Edwards Deming

employees' skills, and innovates ideas leading to enhanced or new products or services.

On the surface, what the team did looked good to them. They were encouraged by meeting their established objective. They thought their measures were okay.

Objective(s) ⟶ Measure(s) ⟶ Act(s) cannot be fulfilled since creditable actions to improve profit will not occur.

Could any of the indicators that were identified, but not used because of the cost, help identify actions that need to be taken? The percentage that time management was involved could be a good indicator, if the target were good (that their involvement should have increased, not decreased). Not having a systematic process for improvement is a major root cause of getting no results. A comprehensive customer satisfaction index could have helped drive improvement actions.

The employee satisfaction indicator could lead to improvement if it is low and a team analyzes what the root causes are and what actions will eliminate them or at least minimize their negative impact.

However, the lack of good principles and the absence of key indicators of corporate performance guarantee that there will be no real favorable results. In the end, no one will be satisfied.

5.7 CASE 2: A STRATEGIC TEAM

5.7.1 The Team's Approach

A strategic team was formed by the company's leadership team. Their charter was to identify what needs to be done to move the company to a continuous improvement environment. The team interviewed the top management personnel as the other team in Case 1. They also set up employee focus groups and several customers' panels. In addition, they developed some customer satisfaction questions to include key attributes such as quality of their products, responsiveness and courtesy of employees, their reliability (ability to keep promises), and the timeliness of delivery of their products. In addition, they decided to benchmark two companies that had recently received awards for their quality improvement achievements.

5.7.2 Preliminary Findings

The team realized that leadership was paramount. Without leadership's commitment, no real improvement would occur. The team recognized that variation to processes was a real problem. They were impressed by several companies' striving to reach Six Sigma quality levels.

Without employee involvement, commitment, and accountability, a continuous improvement program (CIP) is just a bunch of buzzwords. Change is necessary. A whole new philosophy practiced by all employees, including top management, is necessary if the company is to achieve betterment or world-class status. In actuality, a culture change to thinking both strategically and tactically about process improvement is needed. The effort is a journey, not a destination. There is no end; we should continuously get better in all areas such as product design, production, warehousing, delivery, and customer service.

A systematic process for problem solving is essential to achieving significant improvements. Whether the company adopts DMAIC (design, measure, analyze, improve, and control) or focus (measure, analyze, improve, monitor, and take action) the important thing is to have a process that, through training and practice, employees can use in their team efforts and process improvement meetings to solve problems. Coordinating efforts and reviewing progress will be a necessary part of our journey. Communications from top and middle management are an essential element for success. Recognizing achievements and rewarding efforts help maintain momentum.

Customer focus is essential to our business success. Identifying customers' requirements, ensuring that processes always meet or exceed these requirements, and providing world-class service are keys to achieving customer satisfaction.

The team decided to develop the characteristics or guiding principles for implementing a continuous improvement program.

5.7.3 The Guiding Principles

The team identified 10 important principles for CIP. They will be the guiding force to our company in implementing the program and continuing the momentum of improvement.

Guiding principles

1. Top management must be involved. Leaders must be committed to the objectives and goals, provide guidance and support, and recognize and reward achievements.

2. A systematic problem-solving process must be taught to all (in time) and be used in eliminating root causes and reducing process variations. Using data to make decisions should be our way of doing business.

3. Employees must be involved and committed to CIP and be accountable for their actions and responsibilities.

4. Managers and employees must understand why we are implementing CIP, its benefits, their roles and

responsibilities, the problem-solving process, and the new terminology and thinking. Training is essential.

5. Strategic planning is essential for identifying where we are, where we want to go, determining how we are going to get there, and then recognizing when we have achieved our goal. We should turn the PDCA wheel to improve year after year.

6. Process management, including both control and improvement efforts, should become a part of our culture. This concept includes our "daily work."

7. Communications provides the lifeblood of our efforts. Communicate in at least three ways or media to be sure everyone gets the word.

8. Customer focus and satisfaction are our first priority. That's why we are in business and will stay in business.

9. Change, going from where we are to where we want to be, is a normal part of our business environment.

10. Teamwork is essential to achieving continuous improvement. We are in this effort together and together we can achieve world-class status.

5.7.4 Total Wholeness

After identifying the guiding principles, the team developed the concept further.

Need a focus

1. We must develop a good strategic plan that enables us to select a few critical issues/processes that we can achieve better mentor breakthrough.

Process management

2. Once we achieve breakthrough, we manage the process, via control charts or other process measurements.

Improvements

3. If something goes wrong in our processes, we establish teams to solve it or improve it. They will use our systematic problem-solving process.

The team recognized that this is how we should do business. Putting the guiding principles to work and using the discussed ways to do business is how we can achieve success. The team felt that for a company or organization to be "whole," they need to have certain key elements. The team liked the name "total wholeness" because it described that many things must come together if they are to be successful.

Total wholeness

Contains everything to ensure excellent performance and high customer satisfaction.

- A strategic planning and breakthrough focus.

- Customer focus.

- Process variation management.

- Leadership to include visionary and innovation.

- A vendor/input management focus.

- Employee satisfaction.

- Continuous improvement focus (PDCA) includes a problem-solving process and use of data in decision making.

- Measurement of corporate key results and process metrics. Provides linkage to strategic objectives and corporate performance measures.

Now the team was ready to determine which measures they can use to determine how they are doing. First, they asked why the company is taking on a significant improvement initiative. Profit, customers, quality, employee involvement, competition, and growth is why.

5.7.5 Measurement Development

Step 1. Determine the objective

The leadership council spent considerable time on developing objectives. A facilitator led them in this endeavor. A list was developed, prioritized, and then worded into a clear, concise objective statement.

Their List

1. Increase profit by 75 percent in two years.

2. Increase customer satisfaction from good to very good in two years.

3. Improve the quality of our products by achieving Six Sigma levels of our processes in five years.

4. In three years, have 70 percent of our products be recently invented.

5. Develop a culture of continuous improvement by end of next year.

The council ranked item 1 as #1, item 2 as #2, items 3 and 4 as tied for #3, and item 5 last because they believe this would be a by-product of items 2 and 3.

Their statement was rather easy to develop after their ranking and discussion of each item on their list. It was "Increase our profit by 75 percent while improving our customer satisfaction to world-class status in the next two years." Our key outcome metrics are a given. They are:

Now what goes in the blank space to the left? It must reflect measures of efforts that are going to help us achieve our targets (profit and customer satisfaction). To increase profits, we are going to have to increase sales or decrease costs or both. These are both outcome measures. How are we going to decrease costs and/or increase sales? What we are going to do will dictate the other measures we are going to need. Developing the measures themselves does not assure us of success. They just measure whether you make it or not. The strategies and actions produce the results.

Step 2. Traditional Indicators

One of the company's new initiatives is implementing Six Sigma to improve their processes' quality performance. Six Sigma has been and is now being implemented in numerous companies. There have been many books written on the subject. Benchmarking or research will enable the team to identify several traditional indicators in this area.

Cost of poor quality (COPQ), cycle time (beginning to finishing of a process), sigma measure of quality, process throughput, and yield (number produced correctly divided by the total number produced) are some that seem appropriate for this company. Let's review where we are now in our measurement efforts. We have profit and customer satisfaction as measures of our objective.

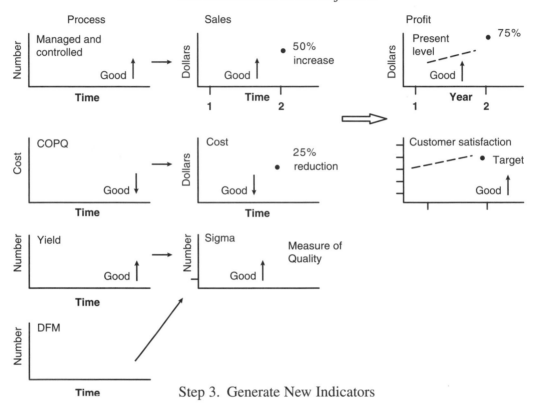

Step 3. Generate New Indicators

In Chapter 3, several methods of generating indicators were outlined. Let's start with process throughput.
What we need are some key process measures.

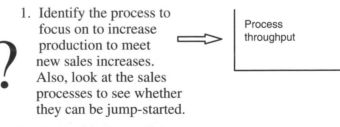

1. Identify the process to focus on to increase production to meet new sales increases. Also, look at the sales processes to see whether they can be jump-started.

2. Determine the technique or method to identify the measures.

Answer:
Flowchart and jump-start methods, Chapter 7

```
            ┌─
            │
      COPQ  │
  ──────────┘

Four costs:

• Internal failure
• External failure
• Prevention
• Approval/inspection
```

Next, let's look at COPQ. In some manufacturing companies, this can run between 20 percent and 40 percent.

Developing this metric takes a tremendous amount of new data not normally collected. It may prove not cost effective. Maybe a different measure can provide similar coverage. The team thought that further study on COPQ should be done to determine the feasibility of collecting the data and the costs versus benefits.

The team also plans to recommend that a "waste or non-value-added" program be initiated to save money. They plan to examine each department and its processes to eliminate waste. Therefore, an activity and an outcome indicator can be useful.

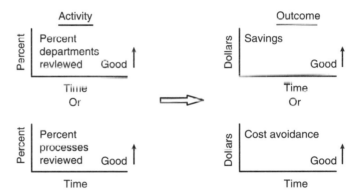

They believe the consultant selected for reducing waste may also help in the metrics development. They developed an action plan for waste reduction.

At closer look, the team thought that maybe the indicator defects per unit might also be appropriate and maybe even amount of rework. Again the best method to get supporting or linking metrics would be to use the flowchart and jump-starting technique found in Chapter 7.

Step 4. Evaluate Indicators

The team evaluated the new indicators that had been generated. Their evaluation follows.

The team felt that percentage of departments reviewed and percentage of processes reviewed basically covered the same thing. Because processes reviewed scored highest, it was selected. However, discussions identified that if we construct the indicator as follows, it will contain almost all of the information of the two (see Figure 5.10).

Step 5. Construct Indicators

The team felt line graphs would be best way to present the data. The graphs would be plotted monthly and would be run-chart type so trends would be evident.

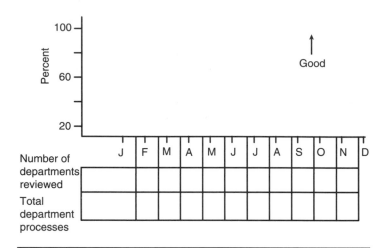

Figure 5.10 Percentage of processes reviewed.

Step 6. Set Targets

Targets were set for profit and customer satisfaction by the leadership team. The other indicator targets would be set after they are baselined with a year's data and studied for how much each needs to contribute so that profit and customer satisfaction can be achieved.

In summary, the team has developed measures and a plan for further study and some countermeasures to impact the metrics. This was an excellent start, but a lot of work remains. The guiding principles and objectives established are sound and would represent that if the organization improved its performance, stockholders/stakeholders would see more profits and customers would be more satisfied.

5.8 SIX SIGMA MEASURES

Between 1981 and 1992, Motorola reported about $1 billion in manufacturing operations savings using Six Sigma. Others, including Honeywell, General Electric, ABB, and Raytheon, reported hundreds of millions of dollar savings (Harry & Schroeder, 2000).

Following are the potentials for saving:

Defect rate parts per million	Sigma level	Opportunities for reduction % of sales
6,810	3	25%
6,210	4	15%
233	5	5%
3.4	6	1%

A simple process can be followed to achieve results.

Step 1. Identify processes, select one by prioritizing by importance and present performances, and determine customers' critical requirements.

Step 2. Develop process flowcharts or maps.

Step 3. Establish key business and process indicators.

Step 4. Review processes versus sigma levels.

Step 5. Use Black Belts and Green Belts to take actions to improve performance.

During this process, management reviews to assess performance progress, promote teamwork and creativity, provide essential support, and recognize and reward successful efforts must be conducted periodically (weekly, monthly, or at least quarterly).

Obvious measures are defect rate "parts per million," sigma level of processes, dollars savings or cost avoidances, customer satisfaction, customer retention, employee suggestions (number and dollar savings), cycle time, and rate of process improvement. These, coupled with other key process indicators and corporate indicators, provide the measures necessary to monitor, to determine where corrective actions are necessary, and to identify improvement opportunities.

5.9 OBTAINING "BUY-IN"

Getting buy-in on a specific performance indicator can be relatively easy or hard. Let's look at what differentiates these two endeavors that are on opposite ends of the scale.

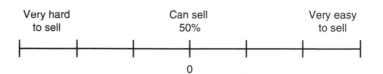

Very easy to sell:

1. A corporate indicator

2. A key process with a metric

   • Meets all good indicator characteristics

   • Has a stretch or realistic target

3. Correlated with customer satisfaction

If PI increases or decreases, customer satisfaction index changes in same direction.

4. Measures an area of high corporate interest or emphasis

For example: The CEO wants meetings to start on time; PI is the percentage of meetings that start on time.

Very hard to sell:

1. Not cost effective to collect data versus perceived value of performance indicator.

2. Measures low-importance process.

3. Does not seem important to the bosses who would review it.

4. Does not meet all "good indicator" criteria.

    In between, it depends on what degree of the very easy to sell conditions it meets. To have any chance to sell, it must meet the "good indicator" criteria. Also, how much the responsible person (champion) of the PI believes it should be implemented can go a long way in securing buy-in. Identifying advantages and disadvantages or benefits and barriers is helpful in selling the performance indicator.

5.10 WHEN TO GET RID OF AN EXISTING PERFORMANCE INDICATOR

1. When it adds no value.

2. Process is no longer used.

3. Process is not as important as it used to be and the measure's costs a lot to maintain.

4. Does not meet all "good indicator criteria."

5. Has not been used or visited by team or process members in a long time (six weeks or greater).

6. When an indicator has the wrong trend and supervision does not believe any action is necessary. (Before deleting, make sure supervisor is right—it could be that action should have been taken.)

5.11 TRAINING/ IMPLEMENTATION PLAN

When a team is appointed to develop metrics, often some training is needed. Some activities/events that should be part of a training plan are:

1. Champion appoints team leader and gets team members approved.

2. Meet with champion.

3. Champion and team leader write charters.

4. Champion gets charter approved.

5. Team meets and formulates plan that includes.

- Objective

- Information needs, internal and external

- Who is going to do what and by when

- Study performance measurement—what it is, how to develop, and how to use it

- Gathers data

    —Interviews of key personnel

    —Holds focus groups or customer panels

    —Researches libraries and company systems

    —Determine whether benchmarking would be useful

- Analyze

    —Perform interviews

    —Turn data into information through analysis

    —Use good indicator criteria

- Make recommendations

    —Make recommendations

    —Develop a force field analysis

    —Use a cost/benefit analysis

    —Sell to appropriate approval level team

Each case will differ to some degree, explaining the need for a customized training plan and implementation plan.

The team should review the activities listed previously and select others appropriate to their charter. The results of this tool will help determine specific training needs. Research the company's ability to provide the training. If training is not available, focus on securing external training. This training will need to be sold to the champion and probably to his or her boss(es).

Put the training plan and implementation plan on a Gantt chart showing what is to be done, by whom, when, and how much time it will take. Monitor how well it is followed and make corrections if needed.

6

Monitor and Take Action: Tools to Improve Your Processes' Performance

6.1 OBJECTIVES

1. Become familiar with a problem-solving process.

2. Learn the key tools/techniques to use during the problem-solving process.

6.2 GLOSSARY

cause-and-effect diagram—A tool to identify potential root causes. Commonly called the fishbone diagram since it looks like a fish. It has the effect or problem in the beginning (at the head), and then four to six major categories of causes are identified and possible root causes are identified for each category.

check sheet—A form designed to collect data. The questions of what, who, why, where, when, and how are asked before the form is designed.

continuous data—Measurable and continuous, such as time. Different control charts are required depending on whether the data is continuous or not.

control chart—A statistical chart that shows whether a process is in control or not. Signals when action is needed. Several types of charts can be used, depending on whether the data is discrete or continuous. Has upper and lower control limits. As long as the occurrences fall within these limits, the process is in normal control (except when trend of seven consecutive occurrences occurs). A particular control chart is selected depending on whether continuous or discrete data is involved.

countermeasures—Solutions that eliminate or minimize root causes to eliminate problem or improve performance.

discrete data—Data that can be counted, such as people.

force field analysis—Helps sell a proposal or solution by identifying the things that will be helpful (pushing for) and those things that must be overcome (pushing against).

graphs—Indicators show where you are at the current situation and results after countermeasures have been implemented. The graphs are mostly run charts, line graphs, column charts, or bar charts.

histograms—A statistical tool to show how data are distributed to select problems or show how the distribution has changed after countermeasures have been implemented. Countermeasures should be feasible (cost effective) and effective (solves the problem). They are actions that eliminate or minimize verifiable root causes.

Pareto chart—A bar chart showing importance in descending order. The most important is plotted first. A cumulative percentage line starting at the beginning and finishing on the last item is constructed. Used as ABC analysis, 80 percent of the problem is caused by 20 percent of the items.

scatter diagram—A tool to stratify problems or events to an actionable level. Helps identify root causes and can be used to develop indicators or identify solutions. First step in determining whether a correlation exists between two variables.

seven original quality improvement tools—The Union of Japanese Scientists and Engineers defines the seven original quality improvement tools as graphs, check sheets, histograms, Pareto diagrams, control charts, cause-and-effect diagrams, and scatter diagrams. Some authors include flowcharts in these categories because they are used extensively in problem solving and performance improvement.

6.3 MONITOR AND DETERMINE ACTIONS

To monitor is to track a performance measure (indicator) and review it periodically to see whether the trend is favorable or not. If not, actions need to be taken by a problem-solving team, root cause teams, or other team (see Figure 6.1).

Measures must be kept current and continuously monitored, and actions must be taken when the measures tell you they are needed. Taking action normally involves developing countermeasures that eliminate or minimize the root causes that made the trend go the wrong way. A problem-solving process is very helpful when a bottleneck occurs or a problem of some kind makes the trend go the wrong direction.

6.4 SEVEN-STEP PROBLEM-SOLVING PROCESS

The seven-step process, flowcharts, and the seven quality control tools will enable you to get a metric back on track or even better than expected. The seven-step process follows closely the plan, do, check, act (PDCA) concept (see Figure 6.2).

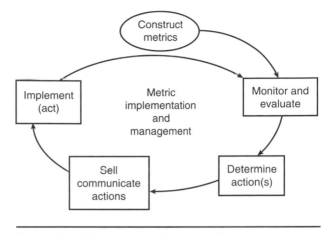

Figure 6.1 Monitor and take action flow.

**7 Step
Metric Development
Process**

1. Identify purpose and establish objective. (Chapter 3)
2. Determine if existing traditional indicators are available and are appropriate. (Chapter 3)
3. Generate new possible performance indicators. (Chapter 3)
4. Evaluate indicators for effectiveness. (Chapter 3)
5. Construct indicator graphs. (Chapter 4)
6. Select targets and plot on graph. (Chapter 5)
7. **Monitor and act. (Chapter 6)**

Step 1. Focus: Identify Improvement Opportunities

Using this technique, there are several ways to identify improvement opportunities. In our case now, where we have a process metric, the bad trend line depicts the improvement opportunity. Teams find improvement opportunities in other ways, including qualitative (brainstorming, nominal group technique), management directions to work on certain problem(s), and quantitative ways such as Pareto charts, benchmarking, and histograms. The improvement opportunity is

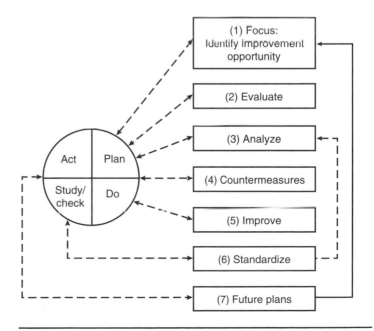

Figure 6.2 Seven-step problem-solving process.

highlighted, a problem statement is written, and an indicator is selected to later show improvement.

Step 2. Evaluate

Once the problem or opportunity is selected, it should be evaluated. A flowchart is normally the best tool to see explicitly what and where in the process the problem is. Also, the metric may need to be stratified to a component that may be more appropriate in measuring success of any countermeasures taken later.

Step 3. Analyze

A good starting point is the construction of a cause-and-effect diagram. The team then should select the most important root causes. Next, the causes should be validated or verified by quantitative methods such as histograms, double Paretos, discriminate analysis, and/or statistical analysis.

Step 4. Countermeasures

For each root cause, at least one countermeasure (solution) should be identified. A countermeasure matrix provides some ranking as to each countermeasure's feasibility and effectiveness. A force field analysis is often useful in identifying what is pushing for the countermeasure's approval and what is against it. A cost/benefit analysis is helpful. Next, the countermeasures normally need to be sold to a higher council that has budget/resource approval.

Step 5. Improve

Once the countermeasures are approved, implementation begins. Coordination and communication are paramount in this endeavor to make sure all affected parties know what is going on in their areas. Project management is used to ensure that projects are on schedule and completed within budget.

Step 6. Standardize

Once the projects are completed, the changes should be standardized (changes in procedures, manuals, and flowcharts). Where the solution involves areas that the project did not address, replication of the solutions should be initiated. For example, one district or regional office may have had a problem that is not reflected in the other offices, but the countermeasures implemented may help them also.

Step 7. Plans

Ask what did we not accomplish or address in this problem-solving project that should be done in the future. Identify what and when on a chart and make it visible to future teams for their consideration.

6.5 THE KEY TOOLS/ TECHNIQUES FOR PROBLEM SOLVING

6.5.1 Introduction

There are key tools available to use in the process. Brainstorming and nominal group technique are covered in Appendices A and B. Measures (including control charts) are covered throughout the book. Certain key tools you need for just about any problem are covered.

6.5.2 Problem Definition

Three most popular methods

1. "Gap–As is" = Problem definition or
   "Gap–Pain" = Problem definition

2. "Pain–Desired state" = Problem definition

Problem definition

40% of the football players are not graduating	or	Only 60% of the football players are graduating on time
Gap		**Pain**
0 – 40%		Not Graduating
As is		**Desired state**
40% of the football players are not graduating		Football players should graduate

Guidelines
1. Don't include solutions as part of the problem statement.
   "There are not enough teachers."
   Implies that if more teachers are added, we will solve the problem.

2. Do not make statements that are too general.
   "Some football players are not graduating."

3. Do not include causes.
   "Playing football takes so much time that players have a hard time graduating."

6.5.3 Data Gathering: Check Sheets

The check sheet is of major importance if the data needed for the indicator are not readily available from a management information system.

Title: _____	Source: _____
Dates included in sample: _____	Other: _____

<table>
<tr><td colspan="2" align="center">Electrical distribution failures</td></tr>
<tr><td align="center">Reason of interruption</td><td align="center">Number of occurrences
from random sample</td></tr>
<tr><td align="center">Lightning
Squirrels
Cable cut
Trees
Other</td><td>THL THL THL THL THL
THL THL 1
THL THL 1111
THL THL THL 1
1111</td></tr>
</table>

All Whats and Hows, but Why?

What is it? A form on which data may be collected and recorded in a uniform manner.

Purpose: Lay out categories of information and data we wish to gather into a format. Categories are determined by asking questions such as:

- What happens?
- Who does it?
- What place, organization, and so forth?
- When does it happen (day, month, hour)?
- How does it happen and how much?

NOTE: Brainstorming items is helpful. Look for stratifications.

Checksheets are one of the seven quality control tools that collects data on who does it, when it was done, how often it occurred, and so forth. In constructing a check sheet, you need to know what you are going to count, when, or where.

Construction:
Horizontally: time period, locations of data you want to check.

Reasons for late SRDs	J	F	M	A	M	J	Total
Customer facility was not ready	11	1	111	1	11	1111	13
Rainy weather	1	1	11	111	1111	111 卌	19
Forgot to schedule	1	11	1	1	1	1	7
Crews on higher priority work	111	1111	1111	卌	11	卌	23
Materials not available	1				1		2
Total	8	8	10	10	10	18	64

Vertically: items, classifications, or categories. Make sure data are accurate and current.

Stratification
Purpose: Break the whole down into actionable elements.

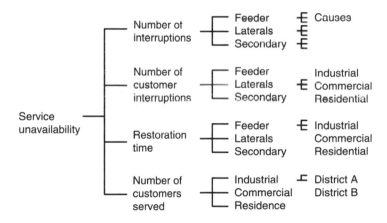

Usefulness:

- • Before developing check sheet

  - – To break the whole into parts that can be addressed by team

  - – To develop an indicator for measuring results

6.5.4 Pareto Chart: Prioritizing

What is it? A chart in which the bars are arranged in descending order from the left.

80-20 rule: 80 percent of the problems results from 20 percent of the causes.

Usefulness: Highlights the "vital few" in contrast to the "trivial many."

Characteristics: Bar touching

Left axis (Y axis) for actual data

Right axis is for percentage of total

Cumulative line from zero

Dr. Noriaki Kano says, "Look for 'fat rabbit' (biggest rabbit, easy to catch) or young 'mountain' (tallest, has not eroded, the one that has the most impact)." That's what you want to address. In the following Pareto chart, it's the lightning.

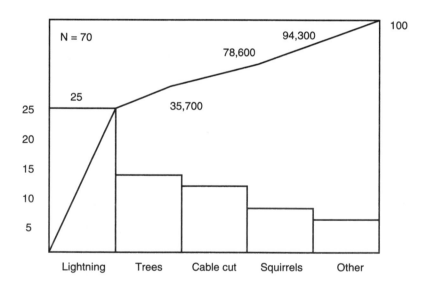

Prioritization:

Products can be prioritized by several categories or criteria:

• Cost

• Number customers impacted

- Gap established by benchmarking, or where you are versus where you want to go

- Savings potential (payback)

- Supports corporate or VP objective(s)

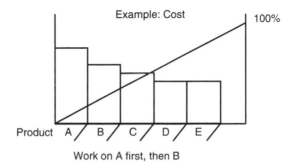

Work on A first, then B

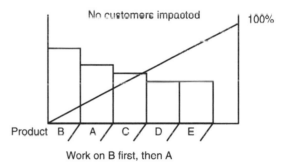

Work on B first, then A

As demonstrated in the previous example, the criteria for product prioritization can and normally will change the selection. When the prioritization has identified the same product with the highest bar in the Pareto, you feel more comfortable about addressing it first.

6.5.5 Understanding the Process: Flowchart

What is it? A graphical representation of a sequence of events to complete a job.

Purpose: It's good practice to draw a job process chart and present it in the front portion of the evaluation of the problem-solving process. Also, it is excellent for using in Step 6, one of the best methods for standardizing procedures or changes in a process.

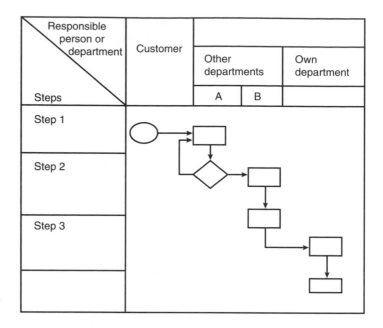

6.5.6 Cause-and-Effect Diagram

What is it? Lines and words designed to represent a meaningful relationship between an effect (problem) and its causes.

Purpose: Identification of potential root causes so that countermeasures can be applied.

Two other common names for the cause-and-effect diagram are the Ishikawa diagram or fishbone diagram.

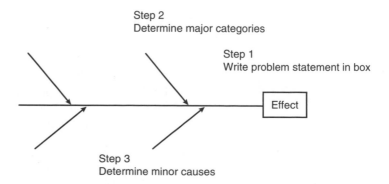

Other uses:
Helps a group or team understand a problem and can show gaps in existing knowledge.

Hints:

Categories (major bones)
First, review the traditional categories:
- Methods
- Machine or equipment
- Material or supplies
- Manpower
- Environment

- Policy
- Procedures
- People
- Management
- Measurement

Second, if you are analyzing a process, draw a flowchart of the process. Next annotate the major process activities. These become the major bones.

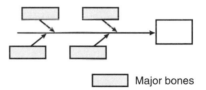

☐ Major bones

Third, brainstorming can help generate the minor bones or have each person write ideas onto a sticky note next to the appropriate major bones.

Fourth, sometimes a Pareto chart is helpful by breaking down the effect of component parts.

Ask:

Why does this occur?
Why does this condition exist?
Complete entire fishbone.

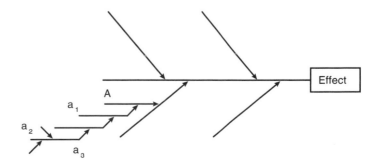

Next cloud the most probable root cause (the last element in the chain) by placing a circle around it.

Using data, verify the most likely root cause(s).

6.5.7 Scatter Diagram

What is it? A diagram that enables you to study the relationship of two variables.

Construction:

Step 1. Collect data and arrange in table (x,y).

Rule ≥ 30 sets of data   The Y axis should be the quality characteristic and the X axis is the factor.

Step 2. For both x and y find the maximum values and the minimum values. Use to determine scale size. Try to keep both scales (lengths) about the same size to make it easier to read.

Step 3. Draw the scale and plot the points.

Step 4. Enter description data on graph: title, source of data, unit of each axis, time period.

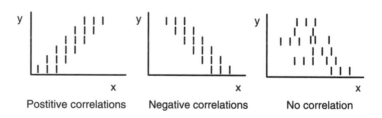

Postitive correlations   Negative correlations   No correlation

6.5.8 Countermeasures Matrix/Force Field Analysis

Purpose: Shows the relationship between the problem, root causes, and countermeasures. Enables the team to select the countermeasures.

Rate each countermeasure from 1 to 5 for its effectiveness and feasibility and then multiply the number in effectiveness

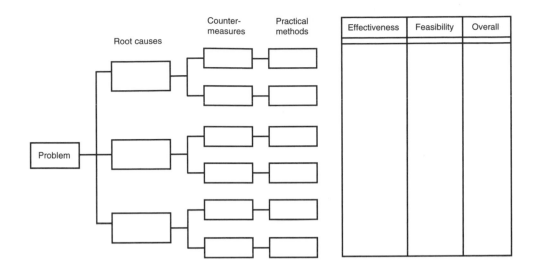

and feasibility by each other and place as the overall score.

1. None   2. Some   3. Medium   4. Very   5. Extremely Well

This ensures that the countermeasures address the most significant root causes.

To help sell the countermeasures, a force field analysis is normally done. Sometimes a barriers and aids is done; it is similar.

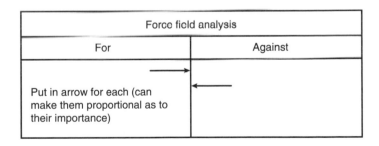

Step 1. Brainstorm list of pushing fors and then a list of things pushing against the countermeasures being sold and accepted.

Step 2. Rank high, medium, and low.

Step 3. Match fors and againsts (if possible).

Step 4. Develop action plan.

Consider factors such as management's will, desire, consistency, savings; cost of implementation, customer's needs, complexity, employees, safety, environment; time/schedule; corporate objectives, and department objectives.

6.5.9 Histograms

Purpose: A visual representation of the spread or distribution of data.

Y axis	Bars proportional in height to the frequency (number of occurrences)
X axis	Class size equal in size

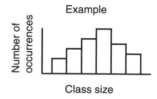

Steps in making a histogram:

$$\text{Data} \begin{array}{ccccc} 3 & 6 & 2 & 5 & 3 \\ 4 & 5 & 8 & 7 & 2 \end{array}$$

Step 1. Range

$$R = \text{Highest} - \text{Lowest}$$
$$= 8 - 2 = 6$$

Step 2. Classes

$$C = \sqrt{n} = \sqrt{10} = 3.16$$

Step 3. Class width

$$W = R/C = 6/3.16 = 1.9$$

Step 4. Unit of measure

$$M = 1$$

Step 5. Round off width and class

$$C = 4 \qquad W = 2$$

Step 6. Lower boundary of first class

$L_1 = Xmin - (m/2) = 2 - (1/2) = 2 - .5 = 1.5$

$L_2 = 1.5 + W = 1.5 + 2 = 3.5$

$L_3 = 3.5 + 2 = 5.5$

$L_4 = 5.5 + 2 = 7.5$

$L_5 = 7.5 + 2 = 9.5$

Exercise:

In a check of 90 footballs, the air pressure varied significantly.

Tallies	Number of footballs	Air pressure (pounds)
1	1	9.25 – 9.5
11	2	9.51 – 9.75
11	2	9.76 – 10.25
ⅢⅡ 11	7	10.26 – 10.50
ⅢⅡ ⅢⅡ ⅢⅡ ⅢⅡ	20	10.51 – 10.75
ⅢⅡ ⅢⅡ ⅢⅡ ⅢⅡ ⅢⅡ 1	26	11.76 – 11.00
ⅢⅡ ⅢⅡ ⅢⅡ ⅢⅡ 1	21	11.01 – 11.25
ⅢⅡ	5	11.26 – 11.50
	0	11.51 – 11.75
1111	4	11.76 – 12.00
11	2	12.01 – 12.25

The upper specification is 11.26 and the lower specification is 10.26.

Is the process capable?

To Do:

Construct a histogram. Use the class intervals given previously.

Calculate the $\overline{X}$ and standard deviation. Then calculate the process capability.

Step 1. Calculate the $\overline{X}$ and S. Set up the following table.

Step 2. Locate midpoint with highest frequency, assign 0 in the u column.

Next, write -1, -2, and so on, toward the smaller observed values while 1, 2, and so on are assigned to the largest values.

Number	Class	Midpoint X	Frequency F	u	uf	u²f
1	9.25 – 9.5	9.375	1	−5	−5	25
2	9.5 – 9.75	9.625	2	−4	−8	32
3	9.75 – 10.0	9.875	2	13	−6	18
4	10.0 – 10.25	10.125	7	−2	−14	28
5	10.25 – 10.5	10.375	20	−1	−20	20
6	10.5 – 10.75	10.625	26	0	0	0
7	10.75 – 11.0	10.875	21	1	21	21
8	11.0 – 11.25	11.125	5	2	10	20
9	11.25 – 11.5	11.375	0	3	0	0
10	11.5 – 11.75	11.625	4	4	16	64
11	11.75 – 12.0	11.875	2	5	10	50
Total			90		+4	278

$u = (x - a)/h$ where a is the midpoint where $u = 0$ was assigned and is the class interval

Step 3. Enter uf and u^2 f in the table.

Step 4. Calculate $\bar{x}$ by the equation

$$\bar{x} = a = h \left(\Sigma \; uf/n \right) = 10.625 + \frac{0.25 \; (4)}{90}$$

$$\bar{x} = 10.62 + .01 = 10.63$$

Step 5. Calculates by using the equation

$$s = h\sqrt{1\Sigma w^2 f - \frac{(\Sigma mf)2/n}{n}} = 0.25\sqrt{278 - \frac{4}{89}} = .25\sqrt{277.955} = .25 \times 16.67 = 4.17$$

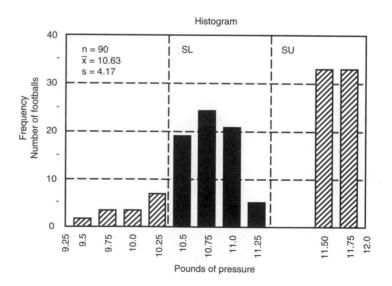

Histogram

$$PCK = \frac{USL - LSL}{66} = \frac{11.25 - 10.25}{6(4.17)} = \frac{1.0}{25.02} = .04$$

Process is yield sensitive and producing a lot of non-forming products. Process is not capable.

6.5.10 Tools/Techniques Summary

Most problems can be solved by using just the seven quality control tools: measures or graphs, check sheets, Paretos, histograms, cause-and-effect diagrams, scatter diagrams, and control charts. Measures and control charts are covered several places in this book. The five other tools were demonstrated in this section; defining problems, stratifications, countermeasures, and flowcharts were also discussed since they are of great use. Matrices and force field analysis were also explained. All of these can be very helpful in problem solving. In fact, the author believes flowcharting should be used in about 95 percent of all problem-solving situations.

The example in Section 6.6 is a simple demonstration of using most of these techniques in a problem-solving situation.

6.6 AN EXAMPLE OF THE PROBLEM-SOLVING PROCESS

This is an example in which a university addresses a problem using the seven-step problem-solving process. Notice that the metric is identified up front and later it shows the results. In the analysis, review how the potential root causes are verified by using data.

Breakthrough University randomly searches its alumni, students, faculty, fans, and community for areas needing improvement. After the surveys were evaluated, the president established three university objectives: improve sports program, increase the courses offered, and beautify the campus. The athletic director was assigned as the coordinating executive (champion) for improving the sports program. Seven thousand people answered surveys; results are shown in the following Pareto chart:

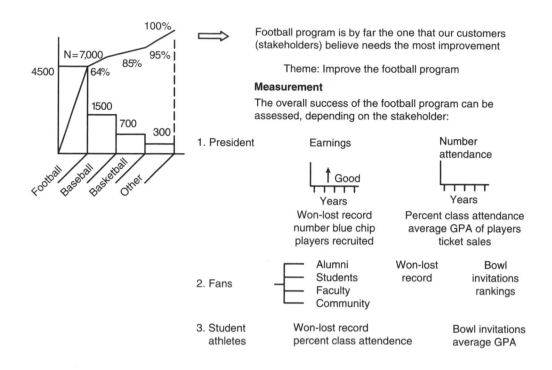

Football program is by far the one that our customers (stakeholders) believe needs the most improvement

Theme: Improve the football program

Measurement

The overall success of the football program can be assessed, depending on the stakeholder:

1. President

Earnings

Number attendance

Won-lost record
number blue chip
players recruited

Percent class attendance
average GPA of players
ticket sales

2. Fans
— Alumni
— Students
— Faculty
— Community

Won-lost
record

Bowl
invitations
rankings

3. Student
athletes

Won-lost record
percent class attendence

Bowl invitations
average GPA

Evaluation

The football coach, with the help of the assistant coaches, established three quality focus areas:

• Victories   • Academics   • Public relations

You have been assigned to support the academic focus area.

Breakthrough University is on the point system:
4.0–A; 3.0–B; 2.0–C; 1.0–D.

The percentages of players by grade are:

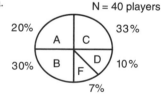

N = 40 players

The customers are the student football athletes. The graduation rate has been:

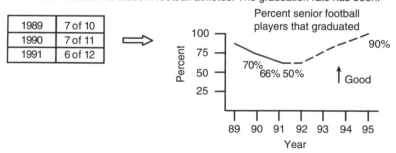

1989	7 of 10
1990	7 of 11
1991	6 of 12

Target: During next four years, achieve 50% improvement to attain a 90% graduation rate.

Problem Statement: During the three-year period, 1989–1991, an average of only 60% of eligible senior football players graduated on time.

Analysis

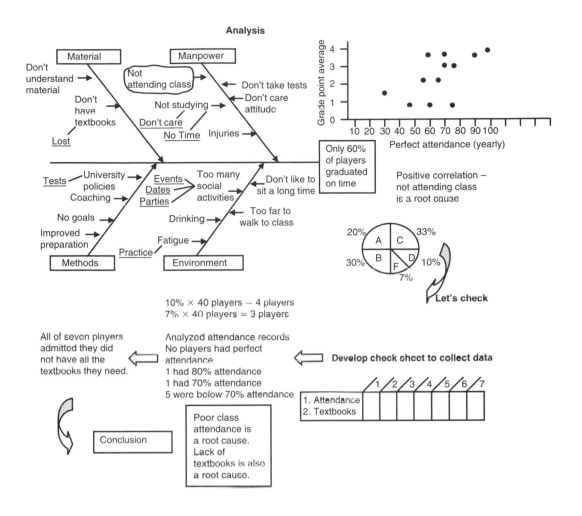

10% × 40 players = 4 players
7% × 40 players = 3 players

All of seven players admitted they did not have all the textbooks they need.

⟸

Analyzed attendance records
No players had perfect attendance
1 had 80% attendance
1 had 70% attendance
5 were below 70% attendance

⟸ **Develop check sheet to collect data**

	1	2	3	4	5	6	7
1. Attendance							
2. Textbooks							

Conclusion

Poor class attendance is a root cause. Lack of textbooks is also a root cause.

Countermeasures

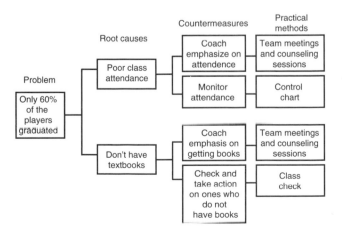

				Effectiveness	Feasibility	Overall
	Root causes	Countermeasures	Practical methods			
Problem	Poor class attendance	Coach emphasize on attendence	Team meetings and counseling sessions	5	5	25
Only 60% of the players graduated		Monitor attendance	Control chart	4	3	12
	Don't have textbooks	Coach emphasis on getting books	Team meetings and counseling sessions	5	5	25
		Check and take action on ones who do not have books	Class check	5	3	15

Barriers	Aids			Implementation plan													
			Who	J	F	M	A	M	J	J	A	S	O	N	D		
• Some don't care	• Coaches recognize importance																
	• Team meetings are periodic	1. Write speech	**Maynard Homack**	—													
• Lazy	• Low cost for implementing																
• Old habits hard to change	• In best interest of all	2. Discuss with coaches	**Maynard Homack**		—												
	• Counseling sessions are an accepted technique	3. Coaches present	**Coach**			—											
• Feel like they are being treated like children		4. Monitor	**Maynard Homack**														
	• Career planning is available	5. Set up and have counseling sessions	**Coach**														

Improvement

Percent senior football players have graduated

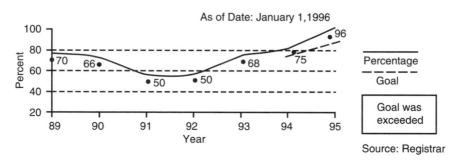

As of Date: January 1, 1996

Percentage
Goal

Goal was exceeded

Source: Registrar

Standardization

Policy

Main goal of student athletes is to get an education.

Student athletes are expected to attend class.

More than 3 absences from class per semester will require an explanation to the coach.

Registrar will monitor and send attendance problem to the coach.

• Policy established
• Communicated
• Monitored
• Check—Action taken

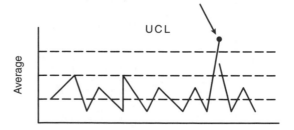

Plans		
	<u>Who</u>	<u>When</u>
Develop computerized exception absenteeism report.	Maynard Homack	By 2nd quarter 1997
Develop and implement textbook receipt quality assurance program.	To be announced	By 3rd quarter 1997

7

Business Processes: Measures and Jump-Starting Daily Work, and Benchmarking

7.1 OBJECTIVES

1. Understand how to develop measures for business processes.

2. Be able to jump-start your processes.

3. Be familiar with benchmarking process (steps) and what to benchmark.

7.2 GLOSSARY

benchmark—A performance level recognized as the standard of excellence for their process.

benchmarking—Process of finding and adapting the best practices to improve organizational performance.

best practice—Best practices are leadership, management, or operational methods or approaches that lead to exceptional performance.

daily work—What functions individuals do each day to earn their paycheck.

enablers—A broad set of activities that help enhance the implementation of a best practice. Enablers explain the reasons behind the performance indicated by a benchmark measure. Enablers help transfer a best practice from one company or organization to others.

jump-starting—Providing the right measures, emphasis, and resources to significantly improve a processes performance.

process owner—The person who coordinates the various functions and work activities at all levels of a process, has the authority or ability to make changes in the process, and manages the process end-to-end so as to ensure optimal overall performances.

135

7.3 PROCESS CATEGORIES

A process is a sequence of activities that produce a product, service, or information.

Process can be classified into three categories. They are key, critical, and sustaining (supporting) processes.

What they are

- Key
- Critical
- Sustaining or supporting

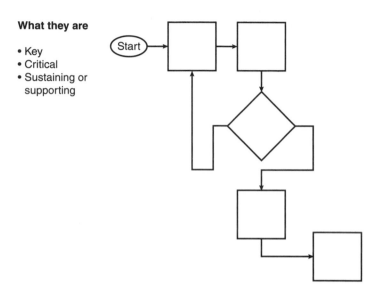

A key process—A major process that has an external customer. When changed, most of organization is affected (normally a cross-functional process).

A critical process—A process that has internal customers; accomplishment of the process ensures the organization's health.

A sustaining or supporting process—Normally functional processes that support either a key or critical process.

These classifications not only facilitate understanding but also provide an insight into their importance.

A business's success will always depend on how well its processes produce. For management to know how well the processes are doing, process and outcome measures must be used and monitored.

Continuous improvement efforts are best accomplished by improving significantly (business process reengineering) or improving continuously (incremental improvements) their key processes. To accomplish either, a terrific tool is the flowchart. It reflects how the process is done (way we do business), who does what, and what we measure (or should measure).

In identifying what to measure, first flowchart the process from beginning to end. Then go look at each activity and question and ask, What should be measured here? And then, Should we measure it? If you plan to measure, put an M reference number such as M^1, M^2, and M^3, by the appropriate question or activity. To demonstrate, take the example of a person selling items on eBay (an online auctioning company).

7.4 PROCESS EXAMPLE: SELLING ON EBAY

First, identify the players (people, systems, and customers). In this case, the process starts with the seller and the other players are the customers, post office, garage sales and flea markets, and the eBay system on the Internet (www.eBay.com).

The flowchart starts with the decision of the seller to go into this business. First, he or she has to get the items to sell, then list them on eBay, answer inquiries about them, notify the customer when they are high bidder and make arrangements for payment, receive payment, package and mail, and review comments and add own viewpoint if appropriate. Each of these could be shown on flowchart as a stage.

Once the flowchart is done, start at the beginning and ask at each activity (a rectangle) and each question (a diamond) whether there is anything at this stage that would be meaningful to know. If so, put an M and appropriate number; then write on the right side what the measure (indicator) would be and your target for the measure. If any indicator measures quality or effectiveness, mark it as Q to distinguish this.

If you understand your process, developing the measures becomes relevantly simple. Don't measure it if it does not help you. Measurement to include data collection takes time and possibly other resources. Do measure if it provides information that enables you to properly manage your process.

This technique can be used on any process from a simple one to a large manufacturing process, service process, or government process. Flowcharting enables you not only to measure the right things, but also to help you identify bottlenecks, waste, or activities that add no value. Streamlining or improving processes should be ongoing in every organization or company.

7.5 DEVELOPING METRICS TO JUMP-START A PROCESS

7.5.1 Metrics Development Example Using eBay

Metrics can drive process performance. If a key process does not have metrics in place to manage by, the introduction of a metric(s) can jump-start the process to achieve the desired performance or results. The philosophy of "what gets emphasized gets done" comes to play here. In developing the metric, it is important that other key activities/tasks are not overlooked or suboptimized. They must be accomplished, but additional focus on the jump-start indicator will lead to improved results. An example of developing metrics to include a jump-start one will be presented.

7.5.1.1 An Example

Many people have jumped on the eBay auction wagon. eBay is an Internet self-merchandising company with 12 million registered users that enables people to sell items online internationally. Some users sell only a few items and others a lot (some as a full-time job).

eBay has a procedure to register users (buyers and sellers). A structured process that is used to list items for sale includes a description and picture of the item. A buyer can select from a list of categories specific items and easily find who has them for sale and for how much. Buyers can easily make a bid. After the specified time period (normally seven to 10 days) is up, the highest bidder is notified that he or she has won the auction. Arrangements are made for the buyer to send the money, including extra for mailing. The seller wraps the item and sends it once he or she receives the money. Feedback to both the buyer and seller allows others to see how they have performed. It provides the seller with an instant credibility rating.

7.5.1.2 Processes

To become a seller, he or she accomplishes the mission by using the following eight processes:

1. Acquiring the items to sell.

2. Getting items presentable and taking their picture.

3. Putting the item description, picture, and other information on eBay.

4. Reviewing progress and answering e-mail inquiries about the item for sale.

5. Receiving the final bid and notifying the buyer of address and postage cost.

6. Receiving payment and banking.

7. Packaging.

8. Mailing.

Each process has several major activities and/or subsystems. Also, they have inputs, outputs, and desired outcomes.

Let's take process: 1. Acquiring the items to sell. The activities and their inputs will vary depending on the methods the process owner chooses. To get items, the individual: (1) already has the item; (2) goes to garage sales to buy items to sell; (3) sells items belonging to others for a percentage; (4) obtains items from friends or relatives; (5) advertises for the items; (6) obtains items from referrals; or (7) buys items from flea markets. The outputs are the items for sale. The desired outcome is to make a profit or achieve some dollar amount of sales in a specific time period.

7.5.1.3 System

The eight processes comprise a system for any seller using eBay to sell products. Each process is important. Hopefully, all are being performed well and the desired outcomes of each are being achieved. However, if any one of the processes is not being achieved efficiently and effectively, it will affect the system results of sales and customer satisfaction. The seller should identify the problem and the root causes and develop solutions that will increase the process's performance.

Often in a process there is one or more activities that, when they receive increased focus (increase the target and develop actions to achieve it), the performance is increased (jump-started). These activities are key to the process's success.

They should always be measured, tracked, and reviewed and corrective action should be taken if needed. Targets or standards provide the emphasis.

The best way to identify these jump-start activities is to first think of the desired outcomes. Next, go into the process and identify the activities that will most likely bring about the desired outcomes. Establish a stretch target for the measure of these activities. By reviewing this for a system (all processes), the manager will often jump-start the whole system if one process's performance is improved (see Figure 7.1).

7.5.1.4 Measurement

Looking at the activities and formulating possible measures is an art (not a science) that one gets better at with practice. Maintaining a desired level of activity in listing items online would be a good measure. If the number of items increases, there is a possibility that the sales will increase.

When the seller knows the average dollars received per item (from history) and the desired "x" sales amount in a week or a month along with the experience of the percentage of items that sell, the amount of items needed to be put on eBay each day to achieve the desired sales can be calculated.

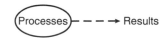

Figure 7.1 System diagram.

By focusing on this activity or process indicator, the system performance can be increased or jump-started.

However, if this activity is to be jump-started, the seller must look backward (toward the beginning of the process or system) to see whether another activity or indicator supports or influences it. In doing so, the activity of obtaining is highlighted. If you are going to jump-start the number of items put on eBay each day, you have to be sure that sufficient items are available to accomplish this. The relevant measure, "number of items available to sell," becomes important.

Other measures (besides the jump-start indicator) should be periodically monitored to be sure everything is going okay. You do not want anything of importance to slip, especially customer satisfaction, measured by the percentage of feedbacks from buyers that are positive. If a problem in any key area is noticed, then the problem should be addressed.

Input (number of items obtained)—**Process jump-start** (number of items put on system)—**Results** (sales dollars and customer satisfaction)

7.5.1.5 Continuous Improvement
Continuous improvement of the processes and systems should be practiced. Also, dramatic process improvements through benchmarking or reengineering should be done as strategic goals or objectives are established.

There are numerous opportunities for achieving continuous improvement. Some examples are:

Process	Possible improvement
1. Getting the items to sell	Teaching others what sells and have them go for you to garage, yard sales and to the flea market.
2. Taking pictures	Have a creative person set up the item display before taking the picture.
3. Putting item's description and picture in eBay	Increasing typing speed. Get a faster computer.
4. Monitoring progress and answering inquiries	Developing some standard answers for often-asked questions.
5. Receiving final bid and providing information	Develop postage cost guide. Set up voice mail and e-mail.
6. Receiving pay and banking	Use PayPal (an online system). Do banking at ATM.
7. Packing	Get boxes free from post office.
8. Mailing	Have mail (including packages) picked up at home.

Once these improvements are made, then new improvements are sought. A plan is developed, implemented, and checked and, if needed, action is taken (remember the Deming wheel).

7.5.1.6 Developing Measures

Although there are several methods of developing measures or indicators, the surest way to having something useful and meaningful is to: 1. define the desired outcome of the system or process; 2. identify measures of success; and 3. select key process measures that significantly affect 1 and 2.

Examples

Process 1: "Obtaining Items."
Step 1. Define the desired outcome: "Find sufficient items cheap that will sell quickly on eBay at a good price."
Step 2. Identify measures of success: "Possible measures of success are: number of items on hand for resale, estimated value of items on hand for resale, number of days production (putting items on eBay) on hand or in inventory."
Step 3. Identify process measures: "Possible process measures are: number of garage sales visited, number of items obtained in a day or at a sale, number items obtained other than garage sale."

Guideline 1: Measures of success must tell how well the desired outcomes of the process or system are achieved. Method: Define first. Then ask, "What has to occur to make this happen?"

Guideline 2: Go into the process to find out what is important to accomplish to achieve the desired outcome(s) and then determine how best to measure. Method: Flowchart the activities in the sequence in which they are accomplished. Look to see what is important to measure.

Guideline 3: Process measures can be numerous. Track only those that are meaningful, because collecting data and tracking expends resources. Method: First make sure they meet the good indicator characteristics. Next, prioritize as to their importance in measuring how well the objective is achieved.

Process 2: "Taking picture of items."
Step 1. Define the desired outcome. "Take an excellent picture quickly that correctly and clearly captures the item."
Step 2. Identify measures of success. Possible measures of success are: 100 percent of items to be put on eBay today have pictures already taken.
Step 3. Identify process measures. They could be the percentage of inventory with pictures taken, percentage of pictures taken correctly the first time, percentage of pictures taken in five minutes or less.

Guideline 4: Normally, percentages provide a better perspective than counts (number of). Most count indicators are not metrics, because they don't necessarily drive improvement actions.

Process 3: "Putting the item on eBay."
Step 1. Define the desired outcome: Put enough items on eBay each day to have a high probability of achieving dollar sales goals.
Step 2. Identify measures of success: Dollar sales per month, percentage put on without any errors, hit-to-miss indicator (percentage of items that get a bid).
Step 3. Identify process measures: They are the number of items put on eBay per day, average number of items on eBay per day, percentage put on without having to redo.

Guideline 5: A balance between efficiency and effectiveness measures should be obtained. In other words, you need both. It is possible to be efficient but not effective or effective but not efficient. Strive to be both. Be efficient in using resources. Seek effectiveness in meeting your objectives and/or targets.

Process 4: "Reviewing progress and answering e-mail inquiries."
Step 1. Defining the desired outcomes: "Be abreast of how sales are going and assure e-mail inquiries are answered quickly with correct information."
Step 2. Identify measures of success: Percentage of e-mail inquiries answered each day. Positive comments in feedback.
Step 3. Identify process measures: Number of e-mail inquiries received per day, average time to review and answer inquiries, time per day spent on this activity.

Guideline 6: When the data are so obvious and available to the seller or process owner and no problems have materialized, tracking data for this indicator (number of email inquiries per day) may not be warranted or beneficial.

Process 5: "Receiving final bid and furnishing buyer with address and postage info."
Step 1. Defining the desired outcome: "Answering on the same day the information for the bidder that enables prompt payment."
Step 2. Identify measures of success: Percent of payments received in 10 days.
Step 3. Identify the process measures: Percentage answered in same day, number of items sold, dollar value of items sold.

Process 6: "Receiving payment and banking."
Step 1. Define the desired outcome: "Receive payments in established time frames and get payments to bank promptly."

Step 2. Identify measures of success: Percentage of payments within 10 days, percentage of payments deposited in 48 hours or less.

Step 3. Identify the process measures: Number of payments late, percentage of late payments for which a follow-up e-mail was sent.

Guideline 7: Often a check list only is needed and a full-blown graph is not warranted. For example, a check mark that payment was made and an annotation of the date would suffice as a measure.

Process 7: "Packing."

Step 1. Defining the desired outcome: "Pack all items so no damage occurs during shipment and within one day of receiving the payment."

Step 2. Identify measures of success: Customer's complaints on packing or damage suffered to item during shipment, percent of items packed and shipped within one day of receiving the payment.

Step 3. Identify the process measures: Average time to pack items, cost of packing, time spent in packing, percentage that have to be repacked.

Process 8: "Mailing."

Step 1. Define the desired outcome: "Mail all packages with 24 hours of receiving payment."

Step 2. Identify measures of success: Percentage of packages mailed within 24 hours, postage variance (received versus paid).

Guideline 8: Customer satisfaction is the most effective measure to track. Feedbacks from buyers provides the seller with how well they are doing. Also getting complaints from customers is excellent if the seller uses the information to improve his or her processes so that increased customer satisfaction occurs and so that buyers trust that they will receive value in both the items they buy and the service they received. These do not have to be graphed by you, because eBay tracks them automatically for you.

The system is composed of these eight processes (see Figure 7.2). The desired outcome is to make money at the established dollar sales target or higher. Also, the desired outcome in customer satisfaction is to include gaining repeat, loyal customers. The measures of success is sales versus target, customer satisfaction, and percentage of complaints. The process measures could be many, but having only three to five would be cost beneficial. The jump-start process measures(s) should always be developed, tracked, reviewed and action taken if needed. Be careful. It is easy to get a "flood of indicators" and many may not be worth the cost of tracking.

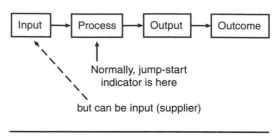

Figure 7.2 Macro process diagram.

7.6 SELECTING THE INDICATORS FOR YOUR USE: AN EXERCISE

Exercise 1: There are numerous possible indicators for you to select from to manage your eBay business. However, if you select too many you will spend too much time collecting and displaying data and not enough on the activities that enable you to make money. However, you cannot ignore the important or key measures that provide you a yardstick of how you are doing versus your goals. You may not need to graph some indicators if the data itself instantly give you the information you need. Check lists, results, counts, and so forth may be examples of this. When you know where you are and the trends are not important, then you may not need to plot on a graph or chart. However, if it is a metric and the trend drives action, then a metric presentation that includes a graph is advisable.

Previously, we identified many possible measures by looking at the activities in a process and identifying the ones that are the most important. We also identified possible outcome measures as measures of success. From this list, what are the ones you would select to manage your eBay business?

Exercise 2: How would this approach apply to any e-commerce business?

7.7 DAILY WORK

7.7.1 Daily Work Performance Measures

For every key process, flowcharts should be created; check lists should be developed for each key activity; and process and outcome measures should be developed and monitored. If the measure shows the wrong trend, it should trigger immediate action by the process owner or process members. Sometimes, the process measure should be a control chart.

7.7.2 Control Charts

Control charts are run charts showing trends and special lines to show whether you have a problem. Control charts are normally in pairs—one to show the average of the process characteristic being measured and one to show the variability (standard deviation, variance, or range).

Using the upper and lower control charts, you can determine whether you have a problem. You plot each point, and

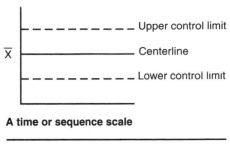

A time or sequence scale

Figure 7.3 Control charts.

as long as they stay within these lines or if no trend in the same direction exceeds six straight points, there is no problem. This goes for both the average and range chart. A plotted point outside of the limits tells us that the process has changed. We now should take some action.

Discrete or continuous data allows for the first decision you need to make to determine what type of control chart is needed. Continuous data is just that: it goes on and on, such as time. Discrete or attribute data is something you can count, such as money or number of cars. There are excellent books on control charts, selection, development, plotting, and when to take action, so full coverage is not warranted in this book. See Figure 7.3 for a typical control chart.

7.8 BENCHMARKING

7.8.1 Introduction

The Air Force's definition of benchmarking is "the process of finding and adapting the best practices to improve organizational performance." A benchmark is "a performance level recognized as the standard of excellence for that process." Benchmarking provides a structure for an ongoing process of measuring and comparing performance. It gives a company or organization an outward focus to find world-class performers, learn from them, and use the information to improve their own performance. It enables an organization or company to set high goals (stretch goals) and have a plan to achieve them.

There are four types of benchmarking (American Productivity and Quality Center, 1993):

Types of benchmarking	
Internal Comparing internally in your organization	**Functional** Comparing within like functions
Competitive Comparing within like organizations	**Generic** Comparing processes to identify best practices

Monitor performance
Adapt changes to
your process or
implement

Prepare to benchmark
Study process
Identify measure
Set goals
Determine who to benchmark

Adapt | Plan

Analyze | Collect

Report and sell
Study
Determine why it is better
Document

Collect performance data
Determine who to benchmark
Conduct on-site visit

Figure 7.4   Benchmarking model.

Before any major benchmarking effort, leadership must be committed to the effort, a team formed and trained, and the process owner involved, and the team must understand the present process and its performance.

7.8.2 Benchmarking Model

A benchmark model similar to the Deming wheel is shown in Figure 7.4.

Numerous benchmark models have been developed: four-step, six-step, seven-step, eight-step, and ten-step.

Before the site visit, study your process; know its activities and the process metrics and outcome metrics you want to improve. Otherwise your site visit will just be a tour.

7.8.3 What to Benchmark?

You should benchmark the processes critical to your organization, such as inventory, production, customer satisfaction, and delivery. A review of major performance measures should show processes needing improvement. Then prioritize by selecting the one most important with the worst performance. This selection will help you decide what type of benchmarking is needed. Look for best-in-class companies such as Disney World, cleanliness and handling a lot of people in a small area (moving lines to events); 3M, innovation; L. L. Bean, distribution; American Express, billing; FedEx, reliability and measuring the key factors of doing business daily; and Air Force, effectiveness. In any event, make sure the company you benchmark is a well-managed company. Direct competitors will not let you benchmark, but someone in your business who is not in your market area may be a good choice for benchmarking.

7.8.4 Sources of Information

Libraries provide excellent secondary research information.

Trade/Technical Journals

Trade and technical journals contain excellent technical information about an industry's products and services. Leading technologies, customer surveys, and research efforts are only a few of the topics discussed.

Government Reports

The Department of Commerce is a primary source of excellent information. The agency publishes news about industrial performance, trends, problems, and success stories about both United States and foreign businesses.

Association Materials/Conferences/Seminars/Round Tables

Industry associations hold conferences and round tables and provide seminars. They also publish materials and excellent magazines, such as IIE's *Solutions* and ASQ's *Quality Progress*.

Databases and Information Networks

These information sources provide invaluable data and insight into other business processes, products, and services and often can be customized to a company's needs:

> NEWSNET—An online service that provides full-text services such as TRW business profiles.

> DRI/McGraw-Hill— Provides online information on global economic and financial information and trends.

> Other sources—There are several other information sources that can be purchased, such as Standard & Poor's Register of Corporations, Directors, and Executives; Principal International Businesses; and Moody's Manuals.

7.8.5 Stating the Model in a Different Way

Benchmarking is, among other things, a measurement and analysis process. Benchmarking can be defined as a continuous process of:

- Identifying (plan)

- Comparing (collect)

- Measuring (analyze)

- Adapting (adapt)

Adapting Identifying

Measuring Comparing

Best practices

Improve organization's performance

Enhance customer satisfaction

The best practices from organizations anywhere can be used to help your organization improve its performance and be more focused toward customer satisfaction.

7.8.6 Benchmarking Is Not

Benchmarking is not:

1. A program—it is a process that works.

2. A substitute for other improvement creativity—it is an enhancing complement to other tools/techniques initiatives.

3. A quick and easy fix—it is a process that requires planning, measurement, comparison, and analysis that upon implementation produces long-term results.

4. Competitive copying or playing catch-up—it is a process of adapting, not adopting.

5. Just data collection and measurement—it is a total process that has a vision, planning and measurement, and implementation of ongoing management reviews.

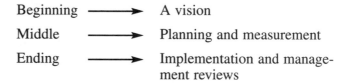

Beginning	⟶	A vision
Middle	⟶	Planning and measurement
Ending	⟶	Implementation and management reviews

7.8.7 Reasons for Benchmarking

Benchmarking provides an opportunity to understand and improve your processes' efficiency and effectiveness. It helps create a sense of urgency and the motivation to improve whatever is essential for survival. It allows managers and supervisors to see how others perform similar processes better. Benchmarking also promotes understanding of world-class performance and provides an excellent focus on customers' needs.

Benchmarking should be undertaken when key performance indicators are not showing "best in class" or "world class," or when relationships and interactions of processes and activities cannot be easily explained or understood because of their complexity, or when complacency has replaced initiative. Benchmarking, like other improvement initiatives, must have commitment from the top down. For one reason, it is not cheap. It will require some resources, but the benefits may be enormous.

Look for processes or programs that are important to the success of your organization. The areas that cause problems or the performance indicators that need a lot of attention are indications of where to benchmark. Other good candidates are performance measures related to the organization's critical success factors such as product development cycle time, distribution and delivery, strategic planning process, maintenance practices, and customer service systems.

7.8.8 Four Methods to Determine What to Benchmark

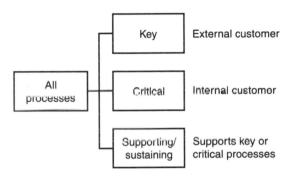

Method 1: Ranking by established criteria

Step 1. Determine importance
Step 2. Assess amount of improvement needed
Step 3. Develop importance vs performance grid

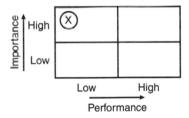

Method 2: Ranking by 3 criteria

Strategic plan

Vision	KRA	Goals	Objective

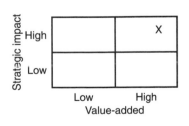

Step 1. Rank strategic objectives as to importance/impacting goals, KRAS, and vision
Step 2. Assess the important ones to see where improvement, potential (value-added) io

Method 3: Rank of goals/processes

Goal/Process

Most Important	1.
	2.
	3.
	4.
	5.
Least	6.
Important	7.

Method 4: Rank against other key criteria

Goal

1.
2.
3.
4.
5.
6.
7.

Or

Process

1.
2.
3.
4.
5.
6.
7.

	Process	Organizational impact	Time	Risk	Cost
1.					
2.					
3.					
4.					
5.					

8

Measuring Apples and Oranges

8.1 OBJECTIVES

1. Learn how to use the objectives matrix.

2. Know when to use a composite indicator and what its advantages and limitations are.

8.2 GLOSSARY

composite indicators—Consists of several indicators rolled up into one indicator. This can be done easily providing each has the same unit of measures, such as percentages, numbers, or averages.

objectives matrix—Rolls up indicators with different units of measures into one composite indicator.

8.3 ONE INDICATOR REQUIRED OR DESIRED INSTEAD OF MANY

Often a manager/executive has so many indicators that he or she desires to have one that tracks how well they are doing.

An example: The manager of a department was developing his department indicators. He felt that if he selected one or two of the most important section indicators and brought them together for his department indicators, he would have a good handle on his major accountabilities and how well he was doing managing them. Therefore, he asked each section to show him their key indicators. The productivity analysis section did not have any functional indicators, so its members sat down and wrote their functions (Step 1).

8.4 AN EXAMPLE

Step 1. In the former construction department of a utility is a small group (two people) whose mission is to administer and implement the productivity analysis incentive programs for two large contractors for the utility's four nuclear power plants. This section is called the productivity analysis section. Their functions/activities were:

- Perform work sampling of crafts at three construction sites.

- Accomplish semiannual contractor performance reports.

- Accomplish work method analysis studies.

- Perform time-lapse photography.

- Administer and analyze foremen delay surveys.

The objectives matrix (Felix, 1983) is the answer of combining indicators of different units into one indicator. It will track how you are doing, but when a problem exists (wrong trend is evident), you need to go to the individual metrics to improve them. This action will improve the one indicator back to an acceptable trend.

Step 2. List the functions and objectives side by side and determine what is important to measure. (If you have a lot of functions, a structure tree can help in doing this.)

Function	What is important	Objective
1. Performs work sampling crafts at the nuclear power plants	Craft utilization (indicator) Many other indicators are possible such as percentage delay time of crafts, percentage waiting time for crafts, and number of work samplings per year. However, craft utilization is selected as the most suitable.	Improve the utilization of the craft assigned to nuclear power plants by 10 percent over a 2-year period. (Discovered this also was the site manager's goal. Also, 10 percent over 2 years is the target for the indicator.)
2. Accomplishes semi-annual contractor performance reports	Twice a year produce a report rating four factors, but "contractor performance" is what is really important. Dollars paid for incentives versus benefits could be potential indicator.	Improve contractor performance by 5 percent (5 percent each year is the target). This was also the vice president's goal.
3. Accomplishes work methods analysis studies	The number of studies could be a measure, but productivity improvement is what is important.	Improve productivity by 10 percent in next 18 months. This was site manager's desire. Formula: $$\frac{\text{Standard hours} \times 100}{\text{Actual hours}}$$ or $$\frac{\text{Output} \times 100}{\text{Input}}$$
4. Performs time-lapse photography	Occurs only once or twice a year—not important enough for measuring.	
5. Administers and analyzes foreman delay surveys	Supports indicators in 1 and 3 above.	

The major thrust of the section is measured by 1–3 and the indicators' selected links (same in this case) to those of higher management.

Step 3. Construct the indicators with targets:

- Contractor performance (rating index)
- Craft utilization
- Craft productivity

Graph strategy				
Recommended department indicators	Type of graph, line bar, improvement/ control	Y axis	X axis	12 MOE average YTD, etc.
Craft utilization	Line (improvement)	Percentage working	Time in months	Monthly
Craft productivity	Line (improvement)	$\frac{\text{Output} \times 100}{\text{input}}$	Time in months	Monthly
Contractor performance	Line (control)	Contractor rating	Twice a year	Semi-annual

Verification or Check

On a scale of 1 to 5 (5 is the most important), rate the importance of the functions:

Functions	Rank	Do we need an indicator?	Do we have an indicator?
Work sampling	5	Yes	Yes
Contractor reports	5	Yes	Yes
Foreman delay surveys	2	No	No
Time-lapse photography	1	No	No
Work methods studies	4	Yes	Yes

The check verifies we are okay. The department manager selected the three indicators ranked as most important. He stated, though, that he would like them to come up with one figure that shows how well they are doing each month.

8.5 OBJECTIVES MATRIX OVERVIEW

The objectives matrix, invented in 1983 by Glen Felix and James Riggs of the Oregon Productivity Center, is the best method of achieving this. It is a composite indicator and used easily for several more indicators than the productivity analysis section has. The rules for formulating the objectives matrix are:

Step 1. Major functions, which could be criteria impacting quality, productivity, or objectives, are identified. Indicators are determined for each and placed in the boxes across the top. See the objectives matrix format in Figure 8.1.

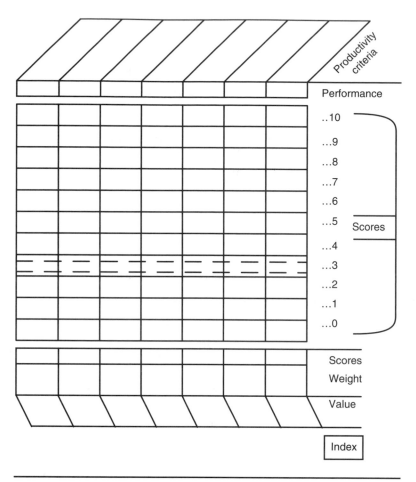

Figure 8.1 Objectives matrix.

Step 1.

Crew utilization	Crew productive	Contractor performance

Step 2. The current level of performance is calculated for each indicator and the numbers entered at a level corresponding to a score of 3 (note that scores are listed vertically at the right). Sometimes current level is listed at a score of 5 (depends on the situation).

Crew utilization percentage	Crew productivity percentage	Contractor performance (1–5)	Scores
			10
			9
			8
			7
			6
			5
			4
40	65	2	3
			2
			1
			0

Step 3. Based on broad organizational goals, indicator objectives are established for all indicators. These quantified targets are entered at a level corresponding to the score of 10. This is where you want to be eventually best-possible performance after taking countermeasures.

Crew utilization percentage	Crew productivity percentage	Contractor performance (1–5)	Scores
70	90	5	10
			9
			8
			7
			6
			5
			4
40	65	2	3
			2
			1
			0

Step 4. Stepwise goals or minor objectives are then determined, and the squares from same levels 3 to 10 are filled in with these successive hurdles.

Crew utilization percentage	Crew productivity percentage	Contractor performance (1–5)	Scores
70	90	5	10
68	85	45	9
65	80	4.0	8
60	77	3.8	7
55	74	3.5	6
50	71	3.0	5
45	68	2.5	4
40	65	2	3
35	60	1.5	2
33	55	1	1
30	50	0	0

Step 5. Because some indicators are more important than others, weightings are assigned to each. The sum of these weights equals 100 and can be distributed in information fashion on the weight row. Previously, we had rated crew utilization and crew productivity each a 5 and contractor performance a 4. Adding the three together, we get $5 + 5 + 4 = 14$. Giving weight for the 5s would produce $5/14 \times 100 = 36$. The 4's weight would be $4/14 \times 100 = 28$.

Crew utilization percentage	Crew productivity percentage	Contractor performance (1–5)	Scores
50	68	2.5	
70	90	5	10
68	85	45	9
65	80	4.0	8
60	77	3.8	7
55	74	3.5	6
50	71	3.0	5
45	68	2.5	4
40	65	2	3
35	60	1.5	2
33	55	1	1
30	50	0	0
36	36	28	Minimum acceptable weight performance
180	144	112	
5	4	4	

Step 6. At the conclusion of every monitoring period (semi-annual because contractor performance is done only twice a year), the actual measure for each criterion is calculated and placed in the performance boxes on row A. The level that these achievements represents is circled in the body of the matrix and associated with a score of from 0 to 10. Scores are entered in the appropriate box on row B at the bottom of the matrix. Each score is then multiplied by the weight for that indicator to obtain a value listed on row C. The sum of all values yields a performance index for the period. Over time, the movement of this single index tracks the net results of performance efforts for the section.

	Crew utilization percentage	Crew productivity percentage	Contractor performance (1–5)	
Row A	50	68	2.5	
	70	90	5	10
	68	85	45	9
	65	80	4.0	8
	60	77	3.8	7
	55	74	3.5	6
	(50)	71	3.0	5 Scores
	45	(68)	(2.5)	4
	40	65	2	3
	35	60	1.5	2
	33	55	1	1
	30	50	0	0
Weights	36	36	28	← Minimum acceptable weight
Row C	180	144	112	
Row B Performance level	5	4	4	Index performance 436

The current level of performance is 50 percent for crew utilization, 68 percent for crew productivity, and 2.5 for contractor performance. These figures are entered in row A. Next, this level of performance and the score circled and the score read from the right and placed in row B (5,4). Then the score for each is multiplied by the weight and placed in row C (5 x 36 = 180, 4 x 36 = 144, and 4 x 28 = 112). These values are summed and put in the index block. This period's overall performance was 436. The highest possible score is row 10's level of performance times the weights or simply 10 x 36 = 360, 10 x 36 = 360, and 10 x 28 = 280, or a total possible index of 1000. (This is the long-range goal.) Next, plot performance on a line graph over time.

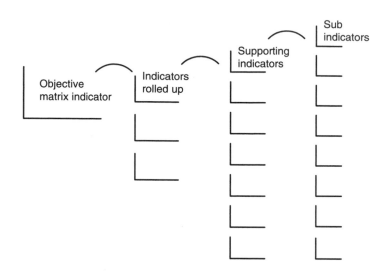

8.6 SUMMARY

If used properly, the seven-step process enables one to roll up all corporate or department indicators into one. The score is reviewed periodically and if not as high as desired, then each indicator included in the objectives matrix is evaluated. If any indicator is not performing to target or standards, actions are taken to identify the root causes and counter-measures are developed and implemented. Often there are indicators supporting these indicators, and you peel them off one by one like an onion to find the problem. Composite indicators for large organizations can be helpful. For small to medium, it is best to display and monitor the individual performance indicators.

9

Customer Focus, Satisfaction, and Measurement

9.1 OBJECTIVES

1. Understand the customer's expectations—what's expected, how to improve the organization's performance, and how to excite the customer.

2. Learn different methods for measuring customer satisfaction.

3. Know how to stratify to get to measurable, sensitive components.

4. Be able to develop a customer satisfaction survey.

5. Review FedEx's excellent system of measuring performance and customer satisfaction in real time.

9.2 GLOSSARY

focus groups—A group of people (five to eight normally) called together by a firm to provide input on new products, service, or customer satisfaction with a product, service, or information.

key thrust areas—The few areas that if emphasized will affect customer's satisfaction the most.

Likert scale—A scale, usually 1 to 7, that enables a customer to rate a company's products and services.

Malcolm Baldrige National Quality Award—The MBNQA is managed under National Institute of Science and Technology and assisted by the American Society for Quality. It developed quality criteria and awards companies annually for exceptional quality in manufacturing, services, healthcare, and education.

RATER—Stands for responsive, assurance, tangible, empathy, and reliability. It was introduced in the film *What Customers Want*.

SQIs—FedEx calls its performance indicators SQIs (statistical quality indicators). SQIs measure performance as it occurs.

survey—Process of asking people their opinions, reactions, ideas, knowledge, and/or requirements.

9.3 CUSTOMER FOCUS

9.3.1 Internal and External Customers

The reason any company or organization is in business is to serve and satisfy its customers. Excellent companies use the customer's voice to improve their processes and the products or services they produce.

Organizations have external customers, who buy their products and/or services. They also have many internal customers. The internal customer is simply one that receives an organizational element's product or services. The warehouse receives finished products from production. The sales department receives inputs from marketing. The production department receives orders from sales. These organizational elements can be both a supplier of the product and services or the receiver of another unit's products and services. Focusing on internal customers can help achieve organizational excellence. Focusing on the external customers enables an organization to survive and thrive.

9.3.2 Dr. Kano's Expectations Model

Dr. Noriaki Kano, a Union of Japanese Scientists and Engineers counselor, produced a model of expectations that states that every product or service has certain expected quality (see Figure 9.1). For example, sheets in a motel must be dry and clean, the air conditioning must work, and

Figure 9.1 Dr. Kano's model of expectations.

hamburgers must have meat. If these basic requirements are not met, the customer will not be happy or satisfied. Improving them does not necessarily improve the customer's satisfaction. But without them, the customer is not happy.

Performance quality is made up of the attributes we measure on customer surveys. If we improve them, customer satisfaction improves. Examples of these are whether the goods arrived undamaged, whether they were delivered on time, whether they were packaged well, and whether the staff was courteous and responsive.

The third category is not known by the customers. Therefore, it is a surprise and exceeds their expectations. Fifteen years ago, some motels started putting shampoo and conditioner in their bathrooms. At that time, most travelers carried their own shampoo if they were going to be gone from home for any length of time. The customers were very pleased about having these small shampoo and conditioners available to them. After a while, customers began to expect them when they arrived at their motel rooms. They stopped carrying their own, and if the shampoo and conditioner were not available, they were very displeased.

Exciting quality is normally provided through employee innovation and sometimes from some customer's recommendations. It produces high customer satisfaction at first. However, over time it becomes expected. New innovations/improvements are needed to maintain that high customer satisfaction.

An organization must ensure that the basic quality requirements are met. Otherwise, they will not be in business long.

Innovations are a key for any organization to ensure success. Creating the climate for innovative/creative people is a goal of any organization reaching to achieve world-class status. Customer panels sometimes can help in this area. Identifying specific customers and bringing them in to discuss their requirements during the design and prototype stages can prove highly beneficial. It will help make sure the final product meets the customer's requirements. Often ideas that lead to innovations are generated.

9.4 MODEL FOR MEASURING CUSTOMER SATISFACTION

9.4.1 The Model

A general model for measuring customer satisfaction is presented in Figure 9.2.

First, the decision to measure customer satisfaction has to be made. Objectives should be established so there is a clear understanding of how the data are to be collected, analyzed, and used.

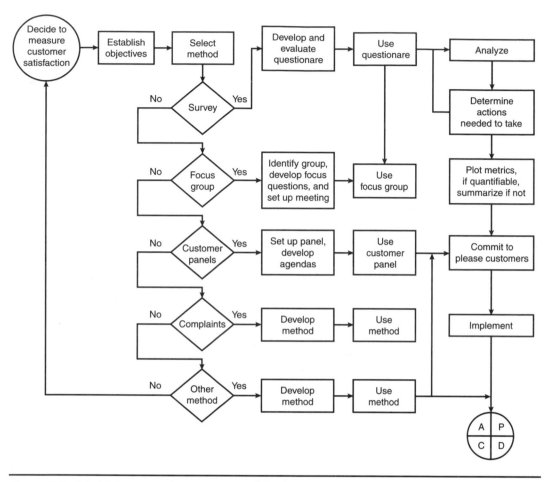

Figure 9.2 Model for measuring customer satisfaction.

Next, the method is selected. Surveys are by far the most used method. Surveys can be handled through focus groups, customer panels, complaints, and other methods. Those methods include comment cards filled out after a customer interaction; poker chips dropped in a box (white: outstanding; red: needs improving); telephone interviews of customers who have recently received a product or services; and numerous other methods.

The number of complaints is an indicator of how well an organization is doing. Hopefully, they will be few in number. Therefore, their value as to how the organization is performing has limited value. The majority of customers will not complain even if they had a bad experience. However, some will tell others, who may not buy your product or service. The real value of complaints is they provide excellent information to be analyzed, root causes identified, and processes improved to make sure the reasons for complaint does not happen again (at least less often). Complaint management, including the collection of the complaints, analysis of them, root cause identification, process improvement, and feedback to the customer is a very important part of customer focus.

9.4.2 Focus Groups

Focus groups have several uses. When a company needs perceptions about a new concept, products, or services, a focus group is an excellent way to obtain this. Also, perceptions about an existing product or services can be obtained. Normally, a focus group consists of five to eight people who have some knowledge of the company or similar products and services. They are invited (by letter) to attend a meeting (approximately four hours in length) in a conference room with a two-way mirror. The two-way mirror allows management, marketing, sales, and production people to observe without bothering the focus members. The group has both a moderator and a reporter. The moderator runs the meeting. He or she prepares the agenda before the meeting and reviews with the company's organization to assure agreement of the approach and content of meeting. The moderator can be from the company, but often is not so that any bias is eliminated. The reporter is normally silent, taking minutes, but can help in writing things on a poster on an easel and so forth. Minutes should be published within five days after the meeting.

The focus group members are often paid a little for their time to include transportation cost. If not, something should be given to them as a remembrance, such as a pen, bracelet, or plaque.

Focus groups can be conducted for other usages. If you have developed a hypothesis and desire to test it, a focus group would be a good method for doing so. This application is called market research. Also, focus groups can provide a good assessment of advertising or promotional concepts, programs, or ideas. They can be used to get interim or immediate feedback on how things are going.

9.4.3 Customer Questionnaires and Surveys

Customer surveys are the primary tools used in identifying how to improve the performance items such as timeliness, responsiveness, and product quality. Because of the importance of customer questionnaires or surveys, most of this chapter will be devoted to their development. We will cover the process for developing surveys, to include determining the attributes to be measured, developing the metrics, and

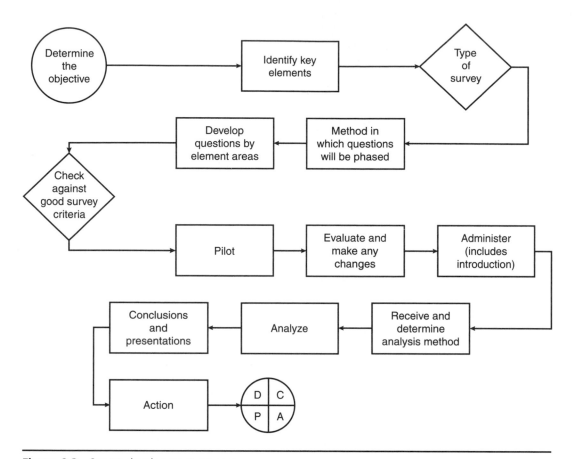

Figure 9.3 Survey development process.

using the results as an input to process improvement and increased customer satisfaction.

A survey development process is presented as Figure 9.3.

9.4.3.1 Objectives
First, determine the objectives. A few possibilities are as follows:

External customers

- Use information to take action to improve our services products, information and/or processes (to drive change).

- Balance cost and customer satisfaction.

- Incorporate customer voice (survey results included in annual strategic planning process).

- Incorporate customer-driven strategies into training and customer service.

Internal customers

- Put in place process or programs that ensure customer satisfaction on an ongoing basis by having departments define their roles as service providers and improve internal service. This will be one of our primary ways to achieve continuous improvement.

9.4.3.2 Random Samples

For a company to use the conclusions of a customer survey with high confidence, the sampling must be conducted random and a particular number of responses must be received. Usual nonrandom surveys response rates are around 30 percent or over and with follow-up 30 percent to 40 percent. These are called block surveys. All you can say is, "A number of participants say that . . . ." Random surveys could call for 80 percent of the random participants to answer if the population were only 100. However, if the populations are larger, the percentage rapidly goes down.

Variance or variability, precision, and confidence levels are very important in determining sample size. The author is going to briefly touch on these. Numerous excellent statistical books on sampling are available at most libraries, and they should be read by anyone planning a comprehensive survey (Hayes, 1997; Kume, 1987).

9.4.3.3 Variability/Precision

If you are measuring customer satisfaction of a group or population that are basically the same types or possess similar characteristics or desires, the sample size will need to be much smaller than if the population consists of several different groups. This is called variability and is estimated by obtaining a small sample. The estimate is called the standard error of sample. This is an important parameter of the formula to calculate sample size of a random sample.

Precision is simply how big is the width of the estimate. We often hear on TV (especially in announcing political polls) as a result between plus or minus points. When they say a customer group is 90 percent satisfied, we need to know the precision (could be ± 10 percent or ± 2.5 percent). That means simply the real answer is either between 80 percent and 100 percent or 87.5 percent and 92.5 percent.

Along with variability and precision, confidence level is important in planning customers' satisfaction surveys (Hayes, 1997).

9.4.3.4 Confidence Level

Confidence levels indicate how sure we are about our findings. Confidence levels of 90, 95, 97.5, and 99 percent are the most used. As confidence level increases, so does the sample size of our survey. A 95 percent confidence level equates to a 5 percent chance of being wrong (a 90 percent chance of being right goes with a 10 percent of chance of being wrong). If you increase by an increment of 2 the chance of error, the sample size must increase by 4. Going from 90 to 95 percent confidence level, increase sample size by 4. From 90 to 97.5 percent, increase sample size by a factor of 16 (Hayes, 1997). Table 9.1 shows the relationship between population size and number of participants needed.

9.4.3.5 Types of Surveys
There are several types of surveys. Mail and telephone are the most prevalent. Comment cards at restaurants, airlines, and retail stores are useful to certain organizations. Interviews are another popular method for determining both internal and external needs. Drop boxes are often employed, using chips, questionnaires, or comment cards. The advantages and/or disadvantages are listed in Table 9.2.

Surveys

- Mail
- Telephone
- Comment cards
- Questionnaires
- Drop box
- Interviews

Table 9.1 Example sample size.

Population size	Number of participants who must respond	
Example: Sample size Requirements 95 percent confidence Chance of error = ± 5 percent		
*100	80	(As population size increases, the percentage of people who have to respond goes down)
400	197	
1000	278	
2000	323	
5000	357	
10,000	370	
20,000	377	

Next, identify key elements. What are the things that are important to our customers about our product or service? Key thrusts/elements are both mission related and customer related. They are normally broad areas such as service, quality, and responsiveness. If done right, they add value to the customer. From these, a customer value map can be used to help identify specific attributes of the product and/or service. An example of an individual who collects items and sells them on eBay will be given to demonstrate how.

9.4.3.6 Customer Value Map
Customer value maps can be used to identify the attributes that should be included for measurement on a customer satisfaction survey (see Figure 9.4).

Table 9.2   Types of surveys and their advantages and disadvantages.

Types	Advantages	Disadvantage	Remarks
Mail	• Relatively cheap. • Easy to administer.	• Low response (30 percent normal). • Some people never fill out first survey received. If they don't get two, they consider it unimportant.	Follow-up (second survey) is normally needed. Sometimes prior to sending survey, a phone call to potential participant asking for their assistance when they receive the second survey will help.
Telephone	• Person-to-person contact; the sound of the answer sometimes implies new information. • Good response rate (over 50 percent) can be achieved by follow-up calls. • Company official can listen in on some calls, if it would be helpful. • Random participation is possible.	• Costly; normally, consulting groups who make telephone survey calls are hired by large companies to conduct them.	Must call at a time the participant is there and not at an inconvenient time. Prelude the survey by telling why you are calling, for whom, and what you plan to do with the results. At the end, thank the participants for their participation.
Comment cards/ questionnaire	• Possible to get good information quickly.	• Cheap method. • Amount of information limited because of size.	Have readily available and convenient to the customers. Humorous answers sometimes help increase the participation rate.
Interviews	• Person to person.	• Very costly to reach a large number of customers.	Must be private. First, make interviewee comfortable. Explain why and how the data will be used.
Drop boxes	• Cheap.	Amount of information is limited.	Be sure method of showing approval such as red chip for dissatisfaction or white for satisfaction is clear.

	Values $\longrightarrow$	Consequences $\longrightarrow$	Attributes
	"The customer's goals and needs"	"What consequences are incurred if the customer value is not met?"	"Product attributes or service behaviors"
Step	Values	Identify	
	Consequences	Identify and join with lines to value	
	Attributes	What attributes or service behaviors of processes that are applicable. Join by lines to consequences	

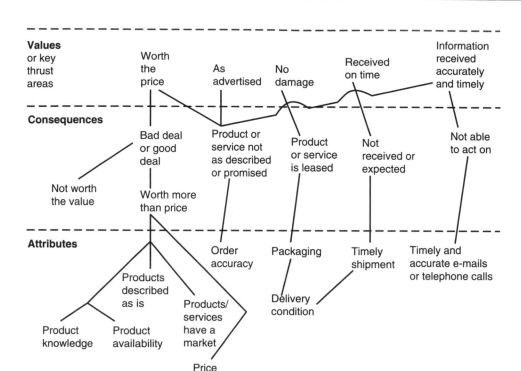

Figure 9.4   eBay customers.

Before the next customer survey, the questions should be rewritten so the answers provide more specific information. It is not unusual for a company to get similar performance on customer surveys year after year and not improve their performance because they did not specifically know what needed fixing. Redesign of questions and the use of customer panels would help alleviate this problem.

If the answer to responsiveness was 4 (very important) and 5 (very responsive), then $P - E = 5 - 4 = 1$ and it is greater than 1. (The customers are very satisfied).

Normally, P–E is calculated for each attribute and one answer on the questionnaire should be designed to be an overall measure of customer satisfaction. For example:

How well do our products and/or services meet your needs? *Needs, requirements,* and *expectations* are useful key words in this question. This is a good overall measure of how the customers feel about your products and/or services. The other questions address specific quality attributes such as courteous representatives and timely delivery.

Customer surveys that include both importance and attribute performance questions provide us with an excellent customer satisfaction measure. Answers to the importance questions become the customer's expectations, and the answers to attributes performance questions are the perceptions. Then P–E becomes our measure. If P is greater than E, we have excellent customer satisfaction. If not, our customers are not satisfied. The latter provides an improvement opportunity. Our problem-solving process with the improvement tools enables us to address this. Sometimes, answers are too vague and don't enable us to know why there is a problem or sufficient to analyze to improve our processes. A customer panel could be formed to address this attribute and provide specifics that can be used to improve performance.

9.4.3.7 Key Thrusts/Common Areas
An organization's products and services do have some common key thrusts/quality dimensions.

Availability: How available are the people in the organization or company? Do they return calls, pick up the phone right away, and answer e-mails? When you need help, are they there?

Responsiveness: How quick do they answer or deliver? Do they help me when I need help?

Timeliness: Timeliness is almost always a top customer requirement. Everyone wants their job done on time, the package delivered as promised, or the project completed on schedule.

Completeness: Everything that was supposed to be done, was done. They were always available, at the beginning until the end.

Professionalism: The staff or salesmen were professional, competent, courteous, showed empathy, and demonstrated a caring attitude.

Satisfaction with Product or Service: The quality of the product was good. It met their expectations or exceeded them. It fits the mission or does what the company claimed it would do.

RATER: Lily Tomlin, in a video called *What Customers Want* (1993) presented a memory pad, "RATER." These five areas are an excellent place

R – Responsiveness

A – Assurance

T – Tangibles

E – Empathy

R – Reliability

to start when you begin writing the survey. It will help you develop the questionnaire topics.

R stands for responsive. Customers expect employees or organizations to be prompt and meet their needs.

A is for assurance. They expect the people who serve them to be competent (know their product or service), courteous (show kindness).

T is for tangibles, the physical things the customers see, such as the facility, cleanliness, safety, and comfort.

E means empathy. Customers want to know the people serving them care (not doing it just for a paycheck) and give them attention and what they want.

R is for reliability, that is, "keeping your promise." If you say it or advertise it, customers expect it from you.

A helpful tool is stratification. Start with quality (could be cost or service) on the left; then go to business processes and finally to customer needs for each output of the processes. Identify any internal metrics that are in place: Sometimes it is apparent what metrics should be in place, even though they do not exist.

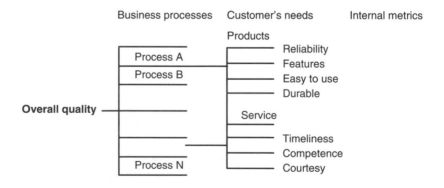

Use a scatter diagram to go from the general attributes to more specific.

Step 1. Customer satisfaction. What do our customers see as value they receive from our company? They see quality product and service, price, and our image.

Step 2. For each of the value attributes, further stratify into more specific quality of product/service such as into delivery, product offerings, and service. Do the same for the other two major attributes.

Step 3. Select from the specific attributes the ones you feel the most important to your customer (use customer panels if possible or sample a few customers).

Step 4. Further break down the specific attribute; for example, delivery can be broken down into contract agreement, on time delivery, countermeasures if something goes wrong, and cycle time changes in product schedule.

Step 5. Do same as Step 3. On-time delivery was selected as the most important. Break on-time down into components that your organization will relate to on-time. In this case, contract agreement, accurate data, and meeting the schedule are the items we need to focus on to ensure excellent customer satisfaction. In developing a customer satisfaction survey, be sure to include the specific and critical items as questions. This enables you to develop questions that are not so vague and broad that customers' answers don't help you improve operations and processes.

Regression Analysis: Adding at least one question (where the customer rates his or her overall satisfaction with your organization's products and services) facilitates the use of regression analysis to determine what attributes contribute the most to their satisfaction.

$$Y = a + b_1 x_1 + b_2 x_2 = t \ldots b_n x_n$$

Overall question on attributes product or service   On-time   Attribute award

The Y is the answers to the overall satisfaction question. The X_s box are the answers to the specific attributes. This tool will provide the attributes most important to the customers.

The following diagram demonstrates the stratification of customer satisfaction. It first asks what contributes value to the customer. The answers in this example are quality, product and service, price, and image (Nauman, Earl, & Giel, 1995). Next, break these down into lower components. For quality of product/service, what adds value? The answer is

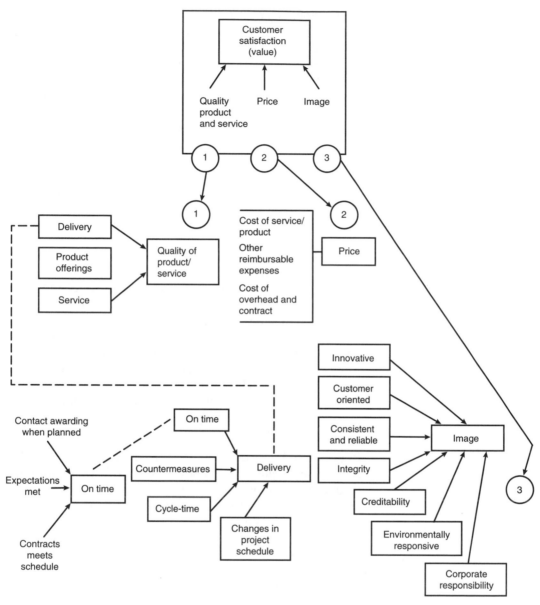

delivery, products offered, and service. For price, cost of service/product, other reimbursable products, and cost of overhead are the lower components. The stratification (breakdown of image) results into seven different components. These components can be further stratified as shown in the quality of product/service's delivery is broken down into on-time delivery, countermeasures, cycle time, changes in project schedule. On-time delivery is further broken down into contracts awarding, expectatons met, and contracts meets schedule. How far should you stratify? To a level, where the components are recognizable in the processes, measured, and corrective action taken when trend is not desired. This technique should be used in all customer satisfaction survey developments to ensure that customers' answers can be transformed to the business processes.

9.4.3.8 Survey Scale Construction

When writing a question containing an attribute, there are a few good rules to keep in mind. Keep it

- Concise, clear, and unambiguous
- No double negatives
- Limited to one thought

There are several methods of using scales (Thursbone, Guttman, and Likert). Likert has a higher reliability coefficient with fewer items than the others. The author has had much better luck with the Likert method than any other.

Likert Type Format: The scale can range from 5 to 7 with 5 being the absolute minimum. Under a 5 scale, you lose significant reliability. The 7 scale has a little more reliability than 5.

To extend scale	1 Not at all	2 To a very little extent	3 To a little extent	4 To a moderate extent	5 To a fairly large extent	6 To a great extent	7 To a very great extent

Frequency scale	1 Never	2 Sometimes	3 Usually	4 Almost always	5 Always		

Agreement scale	1 Strongly disagree	2 Moderately disagree	3 Slightly disagree	4 Neither agree nor disagree	5 Slightly agree	6 Moderately agree	7 Strongly agree

Satisfaction scale	1 Extremely dissatisfied	2 Moderately dissatisfied	3 Slightly dissatisfied	4 Neutral	5 Slightly satisfied	6 Moderately satisfied	7 Extremely satisfied

Reverse answers	1 Very satisfied	2 Moderately satisfied	3 Slightly satisfied	4 Neither satisfied nor dissatisfied	5 Satisfied dissatisfied	6 Moderately dissatisfied	7 Very dissatisfied

A different twist	1 Very poor	2 Poor	3 Neutral	4 Good	5 Very good		

Sometimes a 6 scale is added, such as not observed, non-applicable, outstanding, and so on.

These scales are good for feedback on attributes such as timeliness, competency, courteous, and so on.

The importance scale may look like this:

Importance scale

Not important	Somewhat important	Important	Very important
1	2	3	4

This loses some reliability but may be a little clearer than going to five.

Very unimportant	Unimportant	Half and half	Important	Very important
1	2	3	4	5

Often scales such as below are used in importance performance.

Extremely important

10	9	8	7	6	5	4	3	2	1

Sometimes the answers can be written in a humorous manner (especially good for comment cards). This often increases the participation rate. Example: How did you like the food?

Almost threw up	Tastes horrible	Neither good nor bad	Good	Great- would send others to enjoy
1	2	3	4	5

9.4.3.9 Introduction to Survey

Write an introduction to the survey. Tell how it will be used. State that answers will be kept confidential. Summaries can be provided to the participants.

Most surveys have a low participation rate (30 percent or lower). A clear introduction can help increase this. Other methods are send a second survey with a follow-up letter or call the possible participants. Offer some benefit (a lot of organizations send a $5 bill for participating).

9.4.3.10 MBNQA Example

The Malcolm Baldrige National Quality Award emphasizes the importance of leadership in making progress. The National Institute of Standards and Technology developed a survey to help organizations assess their leadership in relationship to the seven major MBNQA categories (key thrust areas). They wrote a message to leaders (an introduction) before the survey questions.

The MBNQA questionnaire is included as Appendix E.

9.4.3.11 Hotel Example

Following is an evaluation for a hotel (see Figure 9.5). It measures key thrusts/elements (cleanliness, service, food). These types of surveys can be highly beneficial to continuous improvement efforts.

	Good	Fair	Needs improvement
Cleanliness of your room	_____	_____	_____
Working condition of:			
– Television	_____	_____	_____
– Air conditioner/heater	_____	_____	_____
– Hot water	_____	_____	_____
– Lighting	_____	_____	_____
Service of hotel staff:			
– In responding to needs	_____	_____	_____
– Friendliness of employees	_____	_____	_____
– Speed of check-in	_____	_____	_____
– Speed of check-out	_____	_____	_____
Sunrise Restaurant:			
– Quality of service	_____	_____	_____
– Food quality	_____	_____	_____
– Value you received	_____	_____	_____
Ballroom Restaurant:			
– Quality of service	_____	_____	_____
– Food quality	_____	_____	_____
– Value you received	_____	_____	_____

If you were to return to this area, would you stay with us again?

_____Yes _____No

Comments/suggestions:

_____

_____

_____

Name _____ Room number_____

Address _____ Date_____

_____

Group name (if appropriate) _____

Figure 9.5 Hotel example.

9.4.3.12 Entity, Attributes, Goals

On all customer satisfaction surveys, leave a few open-ended questions to allow customers to provide feedback, make suggestions, or praise some efforts. For example:

Please list the three things we need to improve most. What was your most positive experience? What was your most negative experience? Often we need to measure something other than a product or service: a person, place, and event, thing, or even a time period. First, we need to understand what it is we need to measure (subject) for control, evaluate, predict, or to improve. Second, we identify the attributes. A customer value map was used to identify the attributes by first showing the consequences and then the resulting attribute. This same technique can work here or use green-lighting (brainstorming, but not going around table; let everyone speak when recognized through holding a hand up).

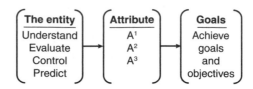

Third, develop the indicator (chart, plot data, and establish the target or goal) (Nauman, Earl, & Giel, 1995).

The survey should include introduction, instructions, attributes questions, importance rating, and room for comments or recommendations.

9.4.3.13 Good Survey Criteria

Ensure that your survey meets these conditions.

1. The survey is as short as possible but long enough to cover the objective's needs. Sufficient attributes to measure you want to be measured.

2. The introduction is clear and compelling, making the participants want to participate.

3. Clear, concise questions are easily understood and not misinterpreted.

4. Instructions tell participants exactly how to fill out the survey and what to do when finished.

5. The survey should be developed so it can be filled out in a reasonable time.

6. A follow-up procedure is in place to notify nonparticipants the importance in their filling out the survey.

9.4.3.14 Pilot, Evaluate, and Change

The survey should be tested on at least 10 people with varying experience to be sure they fully understood the introduction, the instructions, and the questions. Interview each pilot participant to see how they interpreted the questions and whether they had any difficulty in understanding. Ask for recommendations to improve survey.

Incorporate good suggestions into the survey. Feed changes back to the pilot group and ask whether the survey has been improved. Ascertain that no other improvements are needed.

9.4.3.15 Administer, Receive, and Follow Up

Administer the survey in the best manner possible considering cost, feasibility, and effectiveness. Mail surveys are sent by postal service. Telephone calls are normally done right after the area's dinnertime.

Interviews normally are conducted during normal business hours. In some cases, group interviews can be done. Asking a few questions and then having discussions helps the administrator.

Comment cards/questionnaires are administered at the point of sale or as customers leave the premises after using your service. Drop boxes are best where they are noticeable and easy to get to (not crowded into the main traffic aisle).

Once the information is collected, it is categorized and analyzed. If there are areas of concern or needs interpreted, contact the individuals (if possible). Surveys can be conducted with names filled out at the top, or in confidence (no names). Sometimes surveys use no names but numbers; the numbers are associated with companies or organizations.

9.4.4 Internal Customer Satisfaction and Customer Satisfaction Index

The internal customer is whoever receives your products and service. As we try to improve our external customer satisfaction, it is an excellent focus to try to improve our internal customer's satisfaction. Everyone has a customer(s) and all impact the external customers even if it is through another department they serve.

Attributes	Performance		Important		Not observed	Comments
	Extremely good	Very poor	Extremely important	Not important		
1. Responsive – Timeliness – Accessibility	5 4 3 2 1		5 4 3 2 1		N/O	
2. Assurance – Competence – Knowledge	5 4 3 2 1		5 4 3 2 1		N/O	
3. Professionalism – Accuracy – Attitude – Easy to deal with	5 4 3 2 1		5 4 3 2 1		N/O	
4. Empathy – Cares – Courtesy	5 4 3 2 1		5 4 3 2 1		N/O	
5. Reliability – Keeps promises	5 4 3 2 1		5 4 3 2 1		N/O	
6. Overall satisfaction with the products/ services we provide – Provides value – Quality	5 4 3 2 1		5 4 3 2 1		N/O	

Figure 9.6 Internal customer satisfaction survey.

Figure 9.7   Customer satisfaction index.

Surveys, at least annually, are a good way to identify how your internal customers think about your organization's performance and importance. When Florida Power and Light started to implement its quality journey, the power plant maintenance personnel were told the operations department staff were their customers. One individual stated, "That's not right. They are our enemy." Of course, this individual remembers how hard it is to get operations to release a system to them to perform maintenance, receiving complaints of taking too long, and so forth. Once the maintenance personnel accepted operators as internal customers, the personnel were able to identify their requirements. This enabled them to better serve their customers.

An internal customer survey is shown (see Figure 9.6). Both performance and importance are rated. Question 6, overall satisfaction, answers plotted each time a survey is given on a line graph could serve as a customer satisfaction index (see Figure 9.7). Also, gap analysis enables the organization to focus on those attributes that are very important but the performance needs improving.

The customer's satisfaction measurement, tracking, and improvement process is shown in the circle in Figure 9.8.

Figure 9.8   Customer satisfaction, measurement, tracking, and improvement wheel.

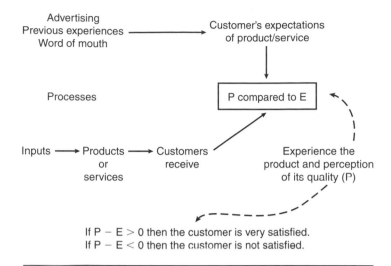

Figure 9.9 Customer satisfaction measurement.

We have covered developing a survey and administering the survey, and now need to focus on analyzing the survey results. From the results, the quality tools are used in solving problems, and recommendations from customers are factored into the improvement process. This is called "taking the customer voice back to improve the organization's or company's processes." The survey method should be accomplished at least annually and a customer index trended over time.

Let's revisit what customer satisfaction is and what the index is.

Survey attributes that are rated by the customers are Dr. Kano's performance quality elements. If we do certain things to improve our performance, the customers' ratings of the attributes will be higher next time. Examples of how we can measure both importance and performance were outlined in the survey development process. Now we will show how this can provide an excellent measurement tool. The examples in Figures 9.9 and 9.10 show how the customer's perceptions and expectations provide us with this excellent measure of customer satisfaction (Nauman, Earl, & Giel, 1995).

Figure 9.10 Gap analysis.

Which one—responsiveness or reliability—would you address first? Responsiveness offers us the biggest opportunity ($5 - 3.3 = 1.7$ compared to $5 - 4.2$ or 8).

Let's say our performance and importance results of our last customers' survey were as follows:

	Importance	Performance
1. Products and services meet needs	4	4
2. Timeliness of delivery	4	3
3. Courtesy of personnel	3	2
4. Competence of personnel	4	2
5. Reliability of personnel (keeps promises)	4	1

Which item(s) would you focus improvement efforts on to improve their performance? Reliability of promises would be the "most important" that needs "the most improvement." Be sure to look at the comment portions of your survey; there should be some specifics on reliability or keeping promises in there.

Next, competence of personnel needs to be addressed. Possibly, specific training needs can be identified.

There is no specific process that works well for every organization. However, there are common activities. Most of the variance comes on how the data is collected from the customers. A company's internal system is then validated by market research, as at FedEx, or generally captured by customer satisfaction surveys, as at major automobile dealers. Comment cards, questionnaires, interviews, and drop boxes are other common techniques. From the customer satisfaction data, an index can be kept over time and periodically updated. The trends will provide the organization or company with how well they are satisfying their customers. Next, a customer satisfaction index is shown as a flowchart model in which a survey method is used to obtain the data (see Figure 9.11.)

Step 10, the customer satisfaction index (CSI), is shown in Figure 9.11. An organization such as FedEx that has developed a system in which the couriers at the customer contact points enter data will generally follow the model to activity 9, 10, or 11 and then execute a few different activities.

Section 9.4.5 focuses on FedEx, which really is the best in class.

9.4.5 FedEx: Measuring Performance and Customer Satisfaction Daily

9.4.5.1 SQIs
FedEx uses statistical quality indicators (SQI) to measure how well it is serving its customers and to identify and eliminate

SQIs

- Measures customer's level of satisfaction from service
- Proactive
- Drives action

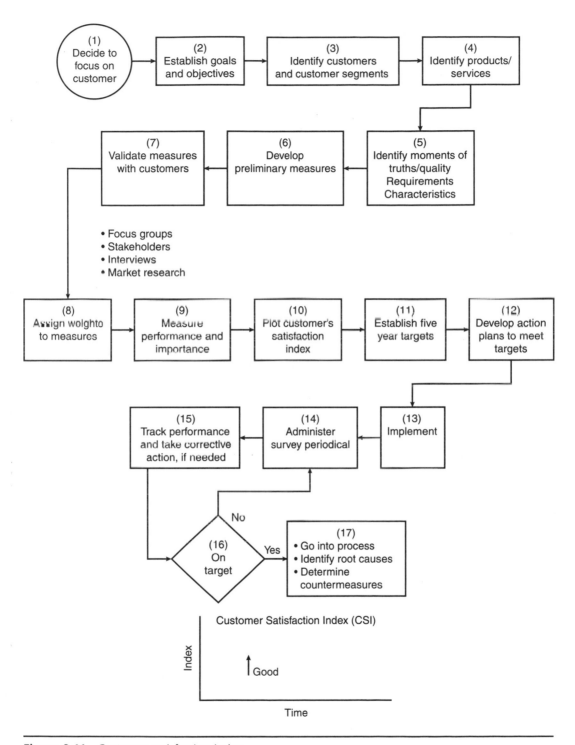

Figure 9.11 Customer satisfaction index.

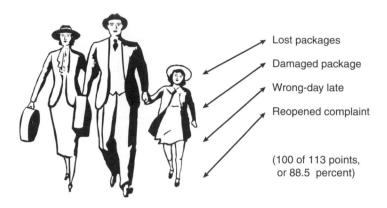

Lost packages

Damaged package

Wrong-day late

Reopened complaint

(100 of 113 points, or 88.5 percent)

Figure 9.12   Customers.

causes of bad performance. Initially, there were 12 separate elements that were measured in SQIs. They were selected because of their perceived importance to the customer. Each element was assigned a weight to reflect the level of dissatisfaction that a failure would create for customers. For example, a package delivered late on the correct day was assigned fewer points than a package delivered on the wrong day (Tsao and Rizwan, 2000).

Several market research studies have been conducted to ensure that SQI measures the service issues that are truly important to FedEx's customers (see Figure 9.12). The results have also been used to adjust the weights assigned to various SQI elements to better reflect the impact a service failure would have on the customer (Rebholtz, 2005).

Over time, several of the elements have been changed/replaced to reflect changes in FedEx operations. For instance, when international operators were expanded, an international SQI element was created.

Also, significant with the SQI measures is that they are usually proactive rather than relative. For example, the measures of late packages (right-day lates and wrong-day lates) reflect all packages delivered late, not just the ones customers contact FedEx about.

See Table 9.3 for the SQIs.

For each SQI, it is absolutely essential to provide an operational definition detailing what should be included and what should not. FedEx does this very effectively. SQIs are the customers' assessment of what is important to them. In other words, they are looking for a company to provide them with a service.

9.4.5.2 Using the System
FedEx's exceptional measurement system has been in place for years. It has enabled the company to improve perform-

Table 9.3 SQIs.
Wrong-day late (WDLs)
Right-day late (RDLs)
Late pickups
Traces
Reopened complaints
Invoice adjustments
Missing proof of delivery (POD)
Damaged packages
Lost packages
Overages
Abandoned calls

ance and customer satisfaction while becoming the world's largest package carrier.

The system is fed by the couriers obtaining information at the pickup and upon delivery. The information updates the system instantaneously, providing all employees the measure of how performance is going right then. When summaries shows problems that were not fixed, teams are formed to solve them.

Because of the size and volume of business, a small improvement leads to a major savings. For example, increasing stops per hour by 0.01 would save $1.1 million per year, and an additional keystroke per package would lose $1.7 million per year (Thomas, 1997).

Daily fixing of problems is possible because the system highlights them and supervisors and engineers jump on the problem and bring them to resolution.

The SQI has 11 components weighted to reflect the customer's view of their performance. To reach its aggressive goals, FedEx has formed a cross functional team for each SQI. A senior executive heads each team and makes sure frontline employees, support personnel, and managers from all parts of the company when needed are involved. Such an action could entail having more than 1000 employees working on problems.

The service goal will always be 100 percent failure-free performance, with emphasis on finding root causes of failure and implementing solutions. The international portions of FedEx use a daily composite to gauge how well they are performing.

FedEx periodically rechecks customer requirements and perceptions and updates its measures and weights accordingly. This ensures that the customer's voice always drives FedEx's actions and processes.

10

Employee Focus, Satisfaction, and Measurement

10.1 OBJECTIVES

1. Learn possible ways to measure employee satisfaction.

2. Become familiar with whom the stakeholders are.

10.2 GLOSSARY

stakeholders—Anyone who has a stake in how well a company or organization performs. Typical stakeholders are customers, employees, stockholders, board of directors, and executives.

Deming Prize—An award for exemplary quality improvement validated by JUSE (Union of Japanese Scientists and Engineers). JUSE established an overseas award, and Florida Power and Light was the first to receive it.

10.3 EMPLOYEE FOCUS

Employees are very important to the success of any organization or company. Employees are one of the key stakeholder groups (see Figure 10.1).

It would seem the other stakeholders, especially customers, could not be highly satisfied with an organization's performance if the employees are not satisfied. Downsizing

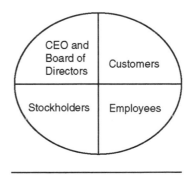

Figure 10.1 Stakeholders.

or rightsizing has lowered morale for many companies, but there has not been a lot of evidence that customer satisfaction has suffered. In fact, boards of directors and stockholders are normally pleased with the lower costs of operations. Employee culture during downsizing changes from company loyalty to one of survival. Often negativity and disharmony results. Deciding who is responsible for what in a new organization is a major challenge. Supervisors and employees are mission oriented and get the job done. Top management can help improve morale by committing to a vision and communicating support. Speeches, in-company TV appearances, and employee panels are excellent communications media for reaching employees. Explanations of why things change and prospects for the future are indeed important subjects. Once employees realize that downsizing is happening everywhere, they accept it better.

Employees realize that they will work for at least three to five companies during their work life. They can no longer expect that their employers will, through loyalty, keep them the entire time of their desired employment. Employees can counter this trend by focusing on their capabilities, increasing their potential (and résumé) through additional training, education, retraining, and new work experiences. Building their résumés has become a priority of most dynamic employees.

Even in this present environment, management can focus on employees' needs by communicating often important aspects and happenings of the company, recognizing and rewarding achievements, deploying improvement powers, providing training, maintaining visible and fair promotion and new jobs programs, and maintaining good health benefits and retirement programs. That people are important has got to be the message of today.

10.4 MEASUREMENT

The most used method of measuring employee satisfaction is employee surveys. They can be administered in groups or can be done on a computer. Likert scale questions provide excellent feedback along with some open questions to give the employees the opportunity to tell it like it is. Employees, like customers, do not like to answer many surveys or questionnaires; about once a year is sufficient. Companies or organizations can obtain quarterly feedback by giving the questionnaire to one-fourth of the employees each time.

The designed survey should focus on what information is important for management. If a company has implemented a new program such as performance pay, empowerment efforts, reorganization, new incentive program, or continuous improvement, it should ask questions about how these programs are doing. Degree of support received from management and supervisors, amount of rework, quality of work, tools to do the job, satisfaction with career progression and/or pay, communications, and visibility of charts and measures are good areas to cover on surveys. Using 15 to 25 questions with a few open-ended questions is normal.

A.
Ideas and openness

Do you have the opportunity to present your ideas to management?

1	2	3	4	5
Never	Sometimes	Usually	Almost always	Always

Authority

Are you empowered with the proper authority commensurate with your responsibility?

1	2	3	4	5
Never	Sometimes	Usually	Almost always	Always

Risk taking and innovation

Is risk taking and innovation encouraged as part of our culture?

1	2	3	4	5
Never	Sometimes	Usually	Almost always	Always

Continuous improvement

How committed are you to continuous improvement?

1	2	3	4	5
Never	Sometimes	Usually	Almost always	Always

Recognition

Do you get properly recognized for your performance?

1	2	3	4	5
Never	Sometimes	Usually	Almost always	Always

B.
Supervision

Does your supervisor support you when needed?

1	2	3	4	5
Not at all	Very little	Moderately	Substantially	Extremely

Happiness with job

Are you happy with your job?

1	2	3	4	5
Not at all	Very little	Moderately	Substantially	Extremely

Happiness with organization

Are you happy to be a member of this division?

1	2	3	4	5
Never	Sometimes	Usually	Almost always	Always

Within three days, the results should be tabulated and analyzed and findings and recommendations developed. Within two weeks, employees should get feedback: findings, conclusions, and changes to be made as a result of the survey. Even if no changes are to be made, give the employees the results and explain why. It is a real morale dissatisfier if the survey is given and then management either ignores the results or does not provide feedback.

FedEx has a well-developed and thoroughly deployed management evaluation system (survey/feedback/action, called SFA). The SFA involves surveys of employees, analysis of work group managers, and a discussion between manager and the work group to develop a written action plan for the manager to improve and become more effective. The survey can be taken online or on paper. In the past, more than 90 percent of all employees responded they are proud to work for FedEx (Rebholtz, 2005).

10.5 SATISFACTION

One of the survey questions should be about employee satisfaction with their job and the company. This index should be graphed quarterly and made visible to all. The title is "employee satisfaction" (see Figure 10.2).

The number of suggestions per employee is a good measure of how engaged the employees are in continuous improvement. Japanese companies have always received a tremendous number of suggestions per employee in their quality journeys. Florida Power and Light, in the successful pursuit of the Deming Prize, received a high level of suggestions from employees (see Figure 10.3).

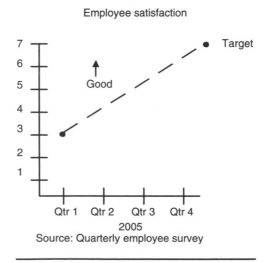

Figure 10.2 Employee satisfaction.

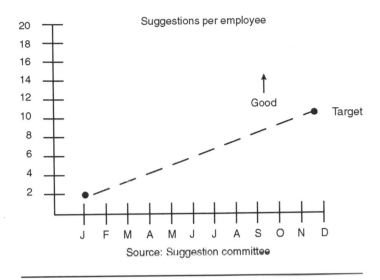

Figure 10.3   Suggestions per employee

Suggestion forms must be simple, available, and easy to fill out and dropped in a convenient location or box. They can be for methods improvements, process improvements, work schedule changes, safety hazards removal, quality-in-work-life changes or additions, and numerous other things encountered by the employees. Develop an indicator and set a realistic stretch target. Keep indicators visible. Be sure that suggestions are reviewed in a timely fashion and that awards and recognition are appropriate and timely. Recognition should be appropriate for the type of suggestion. When the money saved is high, the award should be high; small-change savings should be rewarded with small change, but something employees will be proud to receive.

Employees' participation on continuous improvement efforts shows commitment. Serving on quality action teams, cross-functional teams, and root cause teams is a good way for employees to help solve company problems.

Some companies measure employee absenteeism and believe this is a good measure of employee satisfaction. In reality, a bad absenteeism rate is a strong indicator of dissatisfaction. However, an excellent absenteeism rate may be caused by a lot of reasons other than high employee satisfaction.

Subjective measures, such as reading the climate frequently, cumulating the results, and computing a monthly figure to plot on the climate graph are employed by a few organizations. Walking through the work environment, the manager asks employees, "How are things going?" "Are you happy with how things are going?" "If you could improve one thing, what would you improve?" He or she returns back

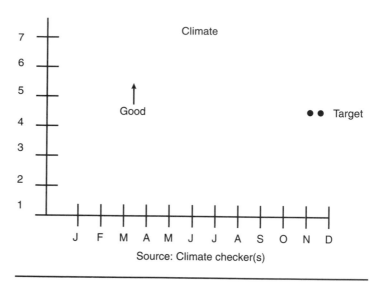

Figure 10.4 Climate.

and judges where on the climate scale the comments placed the climate.

1	2	3	4	5	6	7
Very poor	Significantly below normal	Below normal	Slightly above normal	Significantly above normal	Normal	Very high satisfaction

Each month these are added and divided by the total number of observations, and an index is determined (see Figure 10.4). The index is plotted and monthly targets are set, but they should not influence the "climate checker." He or she must be as objective as possible. Over time, the climate checker will look for key phases and key words. That helps place the climate in the right area. Again, methods of this nature are subjective and may not actually depict degree of employee satisfaction. What it does do is provide leadership by walking around, and this is a positive activity.

When several leaders do climate checks and then come back and reach a consensus through discussions, this provides a better estimate of the climate. Employee surveys are still the best method for assessing satisfaction. They are quantitative and based on frequent and objective answers. Focusing on people is always an excellent management strategy. At FedEx, executive bonuses rest on the performance of the whole corporation in meeting performance improvement goals. In the annual employee survey, if employees do not rate the management leadership at least as high as they rated them the year before, no executive receives a year-end bonus.

11

Designing and Implementing a New Performance Measurement System

11.1 OBJECTIVES

1. Become familiar with the development stages for a new performance measurement system.

2. Learn how to assess metrics awareness throughout an organization.

3. Be able to assess existing indicators and decide which to keep and which to delete.

11.2 GLOSSARY

scorecard—Several indicators measuring, for example, process, customers, employees, and learning and growth; they can be displayed on a computer, made visible on wall charts, and so forth.

team—A group of individuals selected to work together to achieve a desired outcome.

green-lighting—A form of brainstorming that lets anyone give an input, as opposed to going around the room one by one.

11.3 STAGES

Nine stages exist in designing and implementing a new performance measurement system. Sometimes activities may be going on in more than one stage at the same time.

11.3.1 Decision to Go

The decision to have a new performance measurement system can originate from several sources. Customers, employees, top management or leadership councils, middle management, and others can initiate actions. The leadership council (quality council, budget committee, executive committee) will have to approve it. They will be looking for added value. What does it give us we don't have now? How is it going to help us improve? How did we get along all this

Development stages
1. Decision to go
2. Team formulation
3. Understanding present system
4. Deciding what to keep, what not
5. Developing new measures
6. Designing new performance system
7. Implementing
8. Refining

Charter
Objective
Tasks
Expected outcome
Time frame
Team members

time without it? What is it going to cost and is it worth it? These are some of the typical questions. Often the answers are not completely known, so a project officer or manager is appointed to scope it out and present it at a later date. Whether or not approval has been obtained, a team will be needed to ensure proper coverage, knowledge, and development. The team can be in-house or a consultant. If consultant is needed, a statement of work needs to be developed and proposals sought by consulting firms.

11.3.2 Team Formulation

The project manager should also be the team leader. Team members should be selected because of their knowledge, functional area involvement, and interest. Most key processes or functions being measured should be represented on the team. The team likely will be cross-functional. It may be full time or part time. Once the task of designing and implementing a new performance management system is finished, the team is disbanded. The leadership council should recognize them first for their efforts and achievement. Team members can continue to serve as advisors to the system usage and possibilities.

The team should develop a charter that spells out their purpose or objective, tasks needed to be done, time frames, and a statement visualizing the final outcome. Any support or resources needed should be outlined. The charter should be approved by the leadership council.

Next, the team needs to develop an action plan showing who does what, when, where, and how. Team member assignments will be necessary to ensure that the schedule is achieved. If the assignments are part time, a weekly meeting of at least two hours is necessary to assure momentum, focus, and progress. A meeting agenda should be developed (by the project manager) and distributed to each team member two days before the meeting (room number and place, time, purpose of meeting, agenda items to be covered, and so on). Team members should review and bring any information that could be helpful. Of course, the meetings should start on time and end on time. Minutes of meeting should be published within three days after the meeting. The first major thrust should be to understand any performance measurement system that exists.

11.3.3 Understanding Present Measurement System

Almost every organization has some measures, even if most of them are financial ones. Sales, profits, costs, and revenues are almost always available in some format and differing amount of currency (up to date). It is important to identify what is available, because data collection methods are already in place and some of the measures are probably familiar and of some value.

The team or consultant needs to identify what is being measured, the unit of measure, type of graph, formula, data collection method, frequency, users, and perceived benefit or value added. Going from department to department, interviewing process owners, process members, department leads or chiefs, and measurement specialists (if there are any) is one of the best methods. Researching pamphlets, booklets, and presentations is often helpful in identifying what is being measured and what is important to be measured. Attend stand-up progress review meetings and strategic or corporate planning meetings.

Development of a metric knowledge assessment could be helpful in gaining present knowledge. This is simply a Likert scale survey with some open-ended questions or multiple-choice questions that can be administered on a computer or in a called meeting. Explain the purpose, give employees a time limit, answer any questions, and administer the survey. Questions may include:

What measures do you use in accomplishing your job?

- How often do you use or review measures?

- Is your process under statistical control most of the time?

- What is a definition of a metric?

- If you could measure something not presently being measured, what is it?

- What are the strategic performance indicators for the company or organization?

- What are the major strategic objectives of the company or organization?

- What are the key result areas? Which ones do you impact?

These can be written as multi-choice, open-ended, and/or Likert scale questions. An example will follow later. It can be used in assessing anyone's existing metrics system.

11.3.4 Determining What to Keep, What Not

After interviewing, researching, administering surveys, attending meetings, and management reviews, make a list of our findings.

Measure	Units (Y axis)	X axis	Frequency	Data collection who and what	Target yes/no If yes, what	Department use	Process owner	Who uses?	Value

Keep
Improve measure
Stop using

Once the list is prepared, go over it with the team. Make sure everyone understands each measure. Now is the time for the team to be creative. First, what do we keep? Make check marks by the keepers. Next, what can we keep if we improve the existing measure? Finally, mark through the ones we should stop measuring. Consolidate lists into these three categories. Evaluate the first two lists against the good indicator criteria. Use this evaluation to weed out poor measures. Sometimes verification of your findings with process owners is also helpful.

11.3.5 Developing New Measures

After finishing step 6, the team has become fully knowledgeable of the current measurement system in the company or organization. They know what is not important to measure. Going to what is important is a more challenging task. The balanced scorecard offers areas of measurement focus, such as customers, financial, process, learning, and supplier. The company's key result areas are another good place to start. Scott Sink's Seven Indicators—productivity, quality, efficiency, innovation, quality of work life, budgetability, and effectiveness—are another possibility. (Also, the list can be fitted into the balanced scorecard areas: customers, processes, learning, and financial.) Better yet, fit them into such KRAs as quality cost, delivery or schedule, safety, management, people, and so on. These should be the KRAs of the organization. Linkage of indicators from top to lower organization levels can be achieved by using the KRAs. Fit the measures you have to keep and improve into these areas. Determine where gaps (no or little measures) exist. In the latter areas, use the most appropriate metrics development technique, covered in Chapter 3. Then evaluate against good performance indicator criteria. Select the appropriate ones and construct the indicator either manually or on a computer program such as Excel. This should be done before system design. Presentation format design should come out of constructing the new indicators.

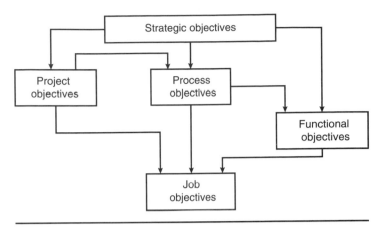

Figure 11.1   Hierarchy of objectives.

Use Figures 11.1 and 11.2 in designing the new system. Depending on the size of the company, which of these indicators will be computerized in a central system will vary.

In all cases, strategic objectives measures will be included. Key outcome process measures are often included. Normally, job, project, and functional measures are not a part of the dashboard computer centralized system (can be on a wall or on a website). However, for large projects, they may be included. In any case, performance measures for project, functional, processes, and jobs should be developed and made visible to those involved.

There are normally many interrelations and support measures that impact higher-level measures. These relationships can be captured in the computer system design and should prove very beneficial (see Figure 11.3).

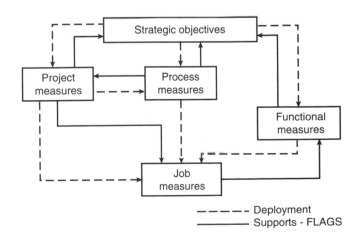

Figure 11.2   Measures provide the linkage: The golden threat.

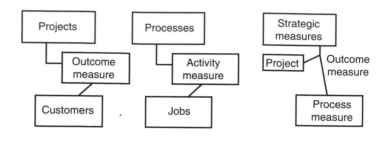

Figure 11.3 Relationships.

11.3.6 Designing the New Performance Measurement System

There are numerous choices in system design, especially in format and presentation of the metrics or measures. Some companies like the measures displayed like the dashboard of a car or plane (see Figure 11.4). All key measures are together, current, and visible, and progress and trends are right in front of you. Posting on paper or electronically in work areas is the preferred display.

Give each trend and its condition state: blue for excellent, green for above or on target, yellow for needs some improvement, and red for needs major improvement.

Computerizing the measure system is the preferred method today. Having the measures in PowerPoint for slide show presentations to leadership councils or management reviews is often practiced. More elaborate systems are also available for multiple uses. Customer's inclusions to company's measures is rapidly growing in popularity. For example, a customer in Europe can determine the status of environmental projects supported by an agency located in the United States by logging on to the system and requesting the programs/project status. Some programmer time will be needed to develop these state of the art systems. Several off-the-shelf (with tailoring to each organization) are available on the market.

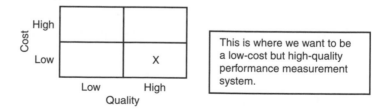

The main characteristic is that the right measure should be current and attainable by the right person at the right time.

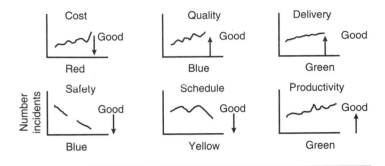

Figure 11.4　Sample instrument panel.

Inquiries or reports should be available in the system, whether online or overnight for large requests.

Remember, even if yours is a small organization, metrics formatted in Excel, tied to a spreadsheet with formulas to calculate measures, are available to almost everyone. The following is a typical presentation format to enable one to select a performance indicator.

	X Corp. PI System
Business operations	
Key processes	PI—0 Introd background
1. Process—Ops	PI—1 Financial
2. Process—Prod	PI—2 Processes
3. Process—Del	PI—3 Customers
4. Process—Ware	PI—4 Learning
Support processes	
1. Process—HR	
2. Process—Acct	
3. Process—Compt	
4. Process—Trans	

When connecting to the system via a web browser, the clients/users should have a user name and a password.

Generating reports and sending them via e-mail and attachments such as spreadsheets and text, presentation formats are defined or can be customized according to users' desires.

11.3.7 Implementing the New System

11.3.7.1 A Pilot

A pilot program should be part of the implementation stage. During the pilot program, debugging, adding, or deleting features should be accomplished. Normally one to three months is adequate time, unless data are highly seasonal.

Small-scale testing of the modules of the system to ensure that there are no bugs is essential. The test should make sure the measurement objectives are met. The system is user friendly, the explanations are clear, customized reports are quickly designed and data retrieved, and the system contains no problems. Calculate the formulas manually; plot the data and check them against the computerized version.

Simulate data and see how the system plots and displays the information and graph. Have the team play around with the system for a few days to see how it performs. Selecting a small group to do the same would help in debugging the system.

At any stage, if the team or consultant feels the budget or approved resources will be exceeded, they must analyze the situation and assess what additional resources will be needed. This determination or request should be presented to the budget committee or resource group for approval before proceeding on the system design.

A detailed implementation plan should be developed to include the pilot, testing, training people in using the system, advertising system availability and uses, and being available for questions or suggestions.

11.3.8 Refining the System

Although we strive for perfection and excellence, things change. Leaders change; customers' requirements and governments change; processes are improved or reengineered; strategic objectives change; and products and services offered are added or deleted. Therefore, we must be ready to refine the system when it is cost effective. Refinement costs are significantly lower than a new system development cost. Make sure any system changes are well thought out, are feasible, and add value. Make changes when they least affect operations.

Online suggestions and/or evaluations of the current system can be made a part of the system. This provides invaluable information needed for refinement decisions. Make it easy for people to suggest refinements, changes.

11.3.8.1 Using the System
Often system design includes a counter that shows the system usage by distinct areas. This is helpful in justifying resources for future needs or refining new systems in the near time.

Training people in what is available, how to retrieve and use it and its limitations, are an impetus to system use. Once the advantages of the new system are evident, system usage will accelerate. Hopefully, system design took this into

Figure 11.5   Essentials for including in new system.

account, and the characteristics of speed, responsiveness, coverage, multiple users, and currency of data were designed into the operations.

Leadership should encourage the use and use the system themselves; setting the example propels acceptance.

11.4 SYSTEM USES

Now with the new performance measurement system in place, the uses of the system are multiple. Organization reviews (such as MBNQA self-audits, management reviews, and management audits) need measures of performance and trends to develop concrete and useful findings. Process performance monitoring to ensure that processes performance meets customer's requirements is absolutely essential in a world-class or best-in-class organization. Measuring progress toward the company's vision or customers' satisfaction are absolutely powerful actions. Project management, including keeping schedules and measures of cost, is necessary for all organizations. Knowing where you stand with all your stakeholders, including your employees, is highly valuable information. Measurement is indeed a major key to success. Without it, you are standing still. No continuous improvement is possible.

11.5 QUICK GUIDE OR TEST FOR NEW PERFORMANCE MEASUREMENT SYSTEM

A guide or quick test for coverage on developing a new measurement system is to ensure it includes the essentials found in Figure 11.5.

If it does include them, the health of an organization can be determined by monitoring and managing these measures. These measures must be current, be visible and easy to access, be inexpensive, be easy to understand, have a data collection plan and reporting method, and have a refinement method available. If you meet these conditions, you should have a measurement system that shows the health of your organization.

12
Conclusion

The importance of measurement and how to use it in strategic planning, process control and improvement, and job measurement were demonstrated.

A seven-step process has been outlined as to how to develop appropriate measures. A comprehensive indicator evaluation instrument was provided to determine whether a potential performance indicator is good and actionable. Eleven methods for generating new performance indicators were outlined, as well as when to get rid of an existing indicator.

Key result areas (KRAs) were covered, and a simple technique to identify any organization's KRAs was presented. KRAs enable any company, business unit, or department in any industry or the military to align their vectors and achieve linkage from the top to where the work gets done.

Processes can be jump-started to increase process performances. A simple explanation of how to achieve this was fully explored using an eBay seller's processes.

Customer satisfaction is paramount to any organization. All organizations exist to satisfy their customers. Measuring how well this is achieved is one of the most important performance indicators that any organization has. Several methods such as surveys, focus groups, comment cards, drop boxes, and telephone interviews were examined. A lot of attention was placed on writing an excellent survey that provides customers' feedback both on performance and importance of critical quality characteristics such as courtesy, responsiveness, reliability, timeliness, and professionalism.

A technique to identify the gap between performance and importance and to prioritize where to put resources for improvement was shown. How to develop internal customers and external customers satisfaction indexes was explained.

Employees are a major stakeholder of any organization. Their satisfaction should be a concern of management, and periodically it should be measured. This measure enables the management of the organization to take corrective action. The next measurement (survey or focus groups) will show whether the actions were effective.

A seven-step problem-solving process was covered, including the key quality tools. A simple quality improvement story demonstrated how the process and the tools can be used to solve problems.

Every company or organization needs a measurement system to manage by. Strategic planning, bringing the customer's voice into the organization to improve its processes and/or operations, and managing processes and jobs are of utmost importance to any organization. Techniques/tools/concepts of how to develop a comprehensive measurement system is discussed and demonstrated where possible.

For each chapter, learning objectives were outlined. If these objectives were met or even close to being achieved, you are ready to approach measurement opportunities with increased knowledge, a process to follow, methods for developing new measures, an ability to measure employee and customer satisfaction, and the skills to lead or be a member on a corporate or business unit measurement team to assess existing performance indicators as well as to recommend new actionable ones. Good luck in your future measurement endeavors.

Appendix A

Modified Nominal Group Technique

- Silent Generation
- Round Robin
- Discussion/Clarification
- Selection

GOALS

1. To increase creativity and participation in group meetings involving problem-solving and/or fact-finding tasks.

2. To develop or expand perception of critical issues within problem areas.

3. To establish priorities, considering the viewpoints of differently oriented groups.

4. To obtain the input of many individuals without the dysfunction of unbalanced participation, which often occurs in large groups.

GROUP SIZE

Similar to QIP Teams size (5–8)

PHYSICAL SETTING

Groups are seated around tables with an easel with a paper pad and magic markers available. Paper and pencil furnished to each participant.

PROCESS

1. Silent Generation

   Write the objectives on the paper pad so they are visible to all participants. Without any discussion, each participant generates lists of ideas relating to the objective (10 minutes; time varies depending on the scope under consideration).

2. Round Robin

   A volunteer in each group acts as a recorder or scribe for that group. He or she asks each participant, one at a time, to present an item, which that person has listed. The items are recorded on the easel paper pad. This continues until each participant's list has been included. Discussion is not allowed, nor should any concern be given to overlapping at this time. "Hitchhiking" is encouraged by having members generate new ideas on their pads, based on items presented by others (at least 10 minutes).

3. Clarification/discussion

   Groups now discuss the items on their sheets for purposes of

   • Clarification
   • Elaboration
   • Additional new items (time depends on scope)

4. Prioritization/Selection

New multivoting is used to determine the top priorities (number varies depending on the objectives). General consensus should be achieved (10 minutes).

Objectives/problems	Impact high/medium/low	Comments
List the indicators • Brainstorm • Nominal group technique • Green-lighting (often you will need more than one indicator)	How well it measures the objective	Does it tell the whole story? Any specifics about the indicator (Existing information, name of system. If not available, difficulty of obtaining.)

Appendix B

Brainstorming

- A technique to encourage creative thinking
- An emphasis on quantity of ideas

RULES

- Clearly state the purpose.
- In sequence, each person takes a turn.
- One thought at a time.
- Don't criticize or discuss ideas.
- Build on ideas of others.

Appendix C

Assessment of an Existing Measurement System

1. Introduction

   Assessment of an existing measurement system can be done in several ways; administering a survey to the appropriate personnel, analyzing, and then verifying the findings is a good method. Another that gets the measurement team more involved and observant is to conduct interviews of the pertinent personnel: department heads, budget review committee, process owners, strategic planners, and so forth. The third method is to use both a survey and interviews. Using the interview method will be described for your use.

2. Interview (about 1 hour each in duration)

   - Vice presidents
   - Department heads
   - Branch chiefs
   - Section chiefs
   - Team leaders
   - Project leaders
   - Quality coordinators/Master Black Belts, Black Belts

3. Find out what metrics (each use), how they are used, how often, and who owns the metric (updates, gathers data, graphs).

For measure's process owner, write name or office symbol. Recap on the Metrics Recap Sheet. Identify the possible uses (process control, improvement, status of programs, strategic objectives, KRA current situation, and others as appropriate to your organization) and appropriate frequencies (daily, weekly, monthly, quarterly, semiannually, annually).

4. Have interviewers make following assessments

   A. Our measurement system is adequate.

   Includes several areas (circle): customer satisfaction, effectiveness, quality, processes, corporate objectives (strategic plan), learning, financial, suppliers, Six Sigma levels, productivity, cycle time, innovation, suggestions savings, and number employee satisfaction.

   B. Measures are linked to corporate measures.

   Yes_____ No_____ Somewhat_____

   C. Most key processes have measures. They are monitored and corrective action is taken when needed.

   Yes_____ No_____ Somewhat_____

   We need to improve our measurement system.

   ①   ②   ③   ④   ⑤
   A lot   Somewhat   Neutral   Hardly   None
                                 any

   _____   _____   _____   _____   _____

   In what areas do we need to improve?

   List _____ _____

        _____ _____

   D. Measures are easy to access.

   No _____
   They are not.

   By computer_____

   On bulletin board or wall in area being measured _____

   Dashboard _____

   Other _____

Yes	Somewhat	No

5. Look for and ensure:

- Measures in departments linked to corporate metrics and strategic objectives.
- Accountability for measures is clear.
- Customer's satisfaction is measured.
- Measures are current and visible.
- Review measures at staff meetings and other important meetings.
- Important data is normally presented graphically.
- Everyone understands the measure(s).
- Doesn't produce a lot of paperwork.
- If measures are not used or don't add value, they are deleted.
- Coverage includes a lot more than just financial measures.

Metrics Recap Sheet

Who _____

Dept _____

Number	Metrics weekly	Objective owner	How used to Improve or control	Frequency (daily, monthly, quarterly, annually)	Metric process/owner

Appendix D

Metrics Awareness Questionnaire

METRICS AWARENESS INSTRUMENT (SURVEY)

Introduction

To assess the metrics knowledge of an organization's people, a questionnaire can be very useful. It can be used also to verify the existing indicator's effectiveness.

Objectives

1. Determine current level of knowledge and frequency of use of the organization's employees with special emphasis on executives, managers, and team leaders.

2. Identify employees' perception of metrics.

3. Identify training requirements, if any, to include specific topic areas.

4. Determine where future metrics development should be directed to achieve increased organization effectiveness.

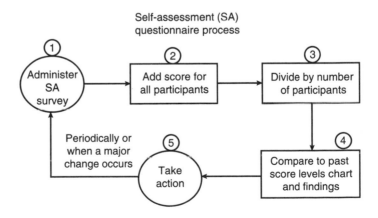

"Take actions" can be:

1. Do nothing; good understanding of measurement.

2. Develop and implement a training program.

3. Do item 2 only where needed, in departments with low scores.

4. Emphasize metrics more in staff meetings or department meetings.

The metrics awareness questionnaire is next. It is formatted so anyone wishing to use it may copy it. The questionnaire is an excellent instrument to determine whether any and what kind of training may be required after the questionnaires. An assessment of existing measures is provided. It can indicate whether a new system is required or just an overhaul.

INTRODUCTION

You have been selected to participate in a Metrics Awareness Assessment. Please answer the questions to the best of your ability. Your answers will not be shown to anyone except the analyst who will tabulate the results.

The assessment tool should take about 30 minutes to complete. Please write your answers using the pencil and answer sheet provided. Thank you for participating. Your answers will help us determine training needs, if any.

METRICS AWARENESS ASSESSMENT

Objectives

1. Determine current level of knowledge.

2. Identify training requirements.

3. Identify employees' perceptions.

4. Pinpoint future metrics needs.

I. Please circle (true or false) most correct answer.

T   F   1. Metrics is an indicator with or without a target.

T   F   2. Most targets are developed using a structured approach.

T   F   3. Metrics should drive action by the process owner or management.

T   F   4. Goals should be specific, measurable, short-term, and realistic.

T   F   5. Effectiveness indicators and outcome metrics are very similar and could be in many instances the same.

T   F   6. Key result areas are the same as critical success factors.

T   F   7. The terms *goals* and *targets* are often used interchangeably.

T   F   8. Productivity indicators are a process indicator only.

T   F   9. The bar chart is an excellent measure for comparing and demonstrating trends.

T   F   10. The measure is located normally on the X or horizontal axis.

T   F   11. Efficiency tells us how well we did in achieving our goal.

T   F   12. Both process metrics and outcome metrics are important to a process owner.

T   F   13. Output and outcome metrics are identical.

T   F   14. Use of range or standard deviation reduction is the most used target setting structured method.

T   F   15. The most important function of a metrics description is to explain how the data should be graphed.

T   F   16. A run chart and a line chart are the same.

T   F   17. Multiple objectives progress should not be plotted on the same chart.

T   F   18. Indicators that contain different measures (apples and oranges) should not be rolled up in a composite index, even if the boss desires just one measure.

I. Please circle (true or false) most correct answer.

T F 19. Ratios are not a good measure.

T F 20. Up to five lines can be easily plotted on a metric, but not an indicator.

T F 21. Counts of inputs to a process is an important and often used metric.

T F 22. A Pareto chart is a special form of a metric.

T F 23. The best chart to show composition of a whole thing is a radar chart.

T F 24. In target setting, set each year's target and sum to determine final objective's goal.

T F 25. A run chart is part of a control chart.

T F 26. A balanced measurement system has an equal number of efficiency and effectiveness metrics.

T F 27. Department should have measures to show how they contribute to the organization's overall vision.

T F 28. Vision should never be reached. "If you get close, raise the bar."

T F 29. Most things cannot be measured.

T F 30. Seldom does just one metric measure one objective.

T F 31. Check sheets, surveys, and data systems reports are the most common way to attain data.

T F 32. Discrete data are best described as something you can measure.

T F 33. A flag system is a system of indicators that show linkage.

T F 34. An action limit is statistically derived.

T F 35. Metrics should primarily be used to control processes.

I. Please circle (true or false) most correct answer.

T   F   36. A zero problem is primarily a reduction objective measure.

T   F   37. More than one measure should never be included on an indicator graph.

T   F   38. A moving average is more accurate than a mean or sample average.

T   F   39. Often supervisors or foremen believe indicators are bad because they are used as hammers against them or they have to spend a lot of time explaining what happened.

T   F   40. Use of data and subsequent analysis of data leads to more superior decisions than years of experience or value judgment.

T   F   41. The mean and medium, but not the variance, are good measures of central tendency of data.

T   F   42. An objectives matrix is used to prioritize alternatives.

T   F   43. An operationalized definition applies to normal operations and does not apply when seasonal data are experienced.

T   F   44. Normalization is an excellent way to make data comparable between organizations.

T   F   45. A 12-month average helps smooth data that include a lot of seasonal data.

T   F   46. Continuous improvement results can best be shown by metrics.

T   F   47. Customers' perceptions can be measured and graphed.

T   F   48. Metrics can be a performance indicator.

T   F   49. Metrics are best developed from understanding key processes.

T   F   50. Some indicators' results can point you in the wrong direction.

II.

A. COPIS model means (please circle correct answer):

    a. customers output performance inputs suppliers

    b. customers operation process inputs service

    c. customers outcomes process inputs service

    d. customers outputs performance information suppliers

    e. customers outputs process inputs suppliers

    f. None of the above

B. Which formula is most correct for productivity?

a. $\dfrac{\text{Output}}{\text{Customer requirements}}$ b. $\dfrac{\text{Output}}{\text{Labor hours used}}$ c. $\dfrac{\text{Input}}{\text{No units produced}}$

d. $\dfrac{\text{Output}}{\text{Input}}$ e. $\dfrac{\text{Input}}{\text{Outcomes}}$ f. None of the above

III.

A. Metrics are (please circle correct one):

    a. Counts of activity   d. Control indicators

    b. Charts   e. All of the above

    c. Meaningful measures

IV.

A. The metrics package includes (please circle correct one):

    a. Operational definition, descriptor, metric philosophy, and data baselining

    b. Operational definition, descriptor, measurement, and key result areas

    c. Operational definition, measurements, descriptors, and graphic presentation

    d. Operational definition, descriptor, graph, and process flowchart

**B. Operational definition includes
(please circle correct one):**

a. Description, customer, equation, and graph
construction

b. Description, target, equation, and indicator

c. Indicator, desired outcome, descriptor, and data
collection plan

d. Description, purpose, descriptor, and
improvement strategy

e. None of the above

ASSESSMENT ANSWERS

1. False
2. False
3. True
4. False
5. True
6. False
7. True
8. False
9. True
10. False
11. False
12. True
13. False
14. False
15. False
16. True
17. True

18. False
19. False
20. False
21. False
22. False
23. False
24. False
25. True
26. False
27. True
28. False
29. False
30. True
31. True
32. False
33. True
34. False
35. False

36. True
37. True
38. False
39. True
40. True
41. True
42. False
43. False
44. True
45. True
46. True
47. True
48. True
49. True
50. True
II. A. c
   B. d
III. C.
IV. A. c
   B. c

(1)	(2)	(3)	(4)	(5)	(6)
Topic areas	Question numbers	Missed	Total possible current answers	(3) ÷ (4) × 100	Needs improvement training Yes No
What are metrics?	1, 3, 5, 8, 19, 21, 22, 26, 27, 29, 30, 32, 35, 36, 39, 40, 44, 46, 47, 48, 49, 50, IIC	Number out of 23	23 × number of participants		
Goals, objectives, and targets	2, 4, 6, 7, 14, 24, 34	Number out of 7	7 × number of participants		
Graph construction	9, 10, 15, 16, 17, 20, 31, 37, 38, 43, 45, IIIA, and IIIB	Number out of 13	13 × number of participants		
Tools and techniques	23, 25, 28, 41, and IIA	Number out of 5	5 × number of participants		
Composites, systems	18, 33, 42	Number out of 3	3 × number of participants		
Categories	11, 12, 13, and IIB	Number out of 4	4 × number of participants		

Sum up the number missed by the question's numbers in the topic areas (1) and (2) and place in column 3. Multiply by the total participants in column 4, divide column 3 by column 4, and multiply by 100 and place in column 5. If column 5 is less than 70 percent in any topic area, this area needs to be addressed by training or emphasized in staff meetings or department meetings (see the Take Actions section).

Appendix E

A Message to Leaders

In today's environment, if you are standing still, you are falling behind. Making the right decisions at the right time is critical. Following through on those decisions is challenging. In a survey of a broad cross-section of CEOs, the Malcolm Baldrige Foundation learned that CEOs believed deploying strategy is three times more difficult than developing strategy. If deployment is so challenging, the questions are, Are you making progress? Would your employees agree? How do you know?

- Are your vision, mission, values, and plans being deployed? How do you know?

- Are they understood by your leadership team? How do you know?

- Are they communicated to and understood by all employees? How do you know?

- Are your communications effective? How do you know?

- Is the message being well received? How do you know?

Are We Making Progress As Leaders? and the companion document for employees, *Are We Making Progress?* are designed to help you know. They provide compatible tools for you to see if your perceptions agree with those of your employees. They will help you focus your improvement and communication efforts on areas needing the most attention. For organizations that have been using the Baldrige Criteria for Performance Excellence, the questionnaires are conveniently organized by the seven criteria categories. For those that have not, this questionnaire identifies opportunities for improvement and directs you to criteria categories that may help you identify some key ideas for making improvements.

It is never too soon to start improving openness and communication. Ask your leadership team to complete this sample questionnaire. It will challenge you to address issues critical to your organization's success.

AN ASSESSMENT TOOL FROM THE BALDRIGE NATIONAL QUALITY PROGRAM

- This new, easy-to-use questionnaire, which is designed to reveal your leadership's perspective, can help you assess how you are performing and learn what can be improved.

- We encourage you to photocopy it and distribute it to your leadership team.

- You can modify the questionnaire to address your specific needs (e.g., add questions, use language specific to your organization).

- You also can download an electronic version of the questionnaire from the Baldrige National Quality Program Web site at www.baldrige. nist.gov. There you may also learn about other program materials, including the criteria, that are freely available to you.

ARE WE MAKING PROGRESS AS LEADERS?

Your perceptions as a leader are important to our organization. There are 40 statements below. For each statement, check the box that best matches how you feel (strongly disagree, disagree, neither agree nor disagree, agree, strongly agree). How you feel will help us decide where we most need to improve. We also have the opportunity to compare the perceptions of our leadership team with those of our employees to see if there are differences (using the *Are We Making Progress?* questionnaire). We will not be looking at individual responses but will use the information from our whole leadership team to make decisions. It should take you about 10 to 15 minutes to complete this questionnaire.

Name of organization or unit being discussed

Category 1: Leadership	Strongly disagree	Disagree	Neither agree nor disagree	Agree	Strongly agree
1a Our employees know our organization's mission (what we are trying to accomplish).	❏	❏	❏	❏	❏
1b Our leadership team uses our organization's values to guide our organization and employees.	❏	❏	❏	❏	❏
1c Our leadership team creates a work environment that helps our employees do their jobs.	❏	❏	❏	❏	❏
1d Our leadership team shares information about the organization.	❏	❏	❏	❏	❏
1e Our leadership team encourages learning that will help all our employees advance in their careers.	❏	❏	❏	❏	❏
1f Our leadership team lets our employees know what we think is most important.	❏	❏	❏	❏	❏
1g Our leadership team asks employees what they think.	❏	❏	❏	❏	❏

Category 2: Strategic Planning

	Strongly disagree	Disagree	Neither agree nor disagree	Agree	Strongly agree
2a As our leadership team plans for the future, we ask our employees for their ideas.	❏	❏	❏	❏	❏
2b Our employees know the parts of our organization's plan that will affect them and their work.	❏	❏	❏	❏	❏
2c Our employees know how to tell if they are making progress on their work group's part of the plan.	❏	❏	❏	❏	❏

Category 3: Customer and Market Focus

Note: Your employees' customers are the people who use the products of their personal work.

	Strongly disagree	Disagree	Neither agree nor disagree	Agree	Strongly agree
3a Our employees know who their most important customers are.	❏	❏	❏	❏	❏
3b Our employees keep in touch with their customers.	❏	❏	❏	❏	❏
3c Their customers tell our employees what they need and want.	❏	❏	❏	❏	❏

	Strongly disagree	Disagree	Neither agree nor disagree	Agree	Strongly agree
Category 3: Customer and Market Focus—cont'd.					
3d Our employees ask if their customers are satisfied or dissatisfied with their work.	❏	❏	❏	❏	❏
3e Our employees are allowed to make decisions to solve problems for their customers.	❏	❏	❏	❏	❏

Category 4: Measurement, Analysis, and Knowledge Management

	Strongly disagree	Disagree	Neither agree nor disagree	Agree	Strongly agree
4a Our employees know how to measure the quality of their work	❏	❏	❏	❏	❏
4b Our employees know how to analyze (review) the quality of their work to see if changes are needed.	❏	❏	❏	❏	❏
4c Our employees use these analyses for making decisions about their work.	❏	❏	❏	❏	❏
4d Our employees know how the measures they use in their work fit into our organization's overall measures of improvement.	❏	❏	❏	❏	❏
4e Our employees get all the important information they need to do their work.	❏	❏	❏	❏	❏
4f Our employees get the information they need to know how our organization is doing.	❏	❏	❏	❏	❏

Category 5: Human Resource Focus

	Strongly disagree	Disagree	Neither agree nor disagree	Agree	Strongly agree
5a Our employees can make changes that will improve their work.	❏	❏	❏	❏	❏
5b Our employees cooperate and work as a team.	❏	❏	❏	❏	❏
5c We encourage and enable our employees to develop their job skills so they can advance their careers.	❏	❏	❏	❏	❏
5d Our employees are recognized for their work.	❏	❏	❏	❏	❏
5e Our employees have a safe workplace.	❏	❏	❏	❏	❏
5f Our managers and our organization care about our employees.	❏	❏	❏	❏	❏

Category 6: Process Management	Strongly disagree	Disagree	Neither agree nor disagree	Agree	Strongly agree
6a Our employees can get everything they need to do their jobs.	❏	❏	❏	❏	❏
6b Our employees collect information (data) about the quality of their work.	❏	❏	❏	❏	❏
6c Our organization has good processes for doing our work.	❏	❏	❏	❏	❏
6d Our employees have control over their personal work processes.	❏	❏	❏	❏	❏

Category 7: Business Results

	Strongly disagree	Disagree	Neither agree nor disagree	Agree	Strongly agree
7a Our employees' customers are satisfied with their work.	❏	❏	❏	❏	❏
7b Our employees' work products meet all requirements.	❏	❏	❏	❏	❏
7c Our employees know how well our organization is doing financially.	❏	❏	❏	❏	❏
7d Our organization uses our employees' time and talents well.	❏	❏	❏	❏	❏
7e Our organization removes things that get in the way of progress.	❏	❏	❏	❏	❏
7f Our organization obeys laws and regulations.	❏	❏	❏	❏	❏
7g Our organization has high standards and ethics.	❏	❏	❏	❏	❏
7h Our organization helps our employees help their community.	❏	❏	❏	❏	❏
7i Our employees are satisfied with their jobs.	❏	❏	❏	❏	❏

Would you like to give more information about any of your responses? Please include the number of the statement (for example, 2a or 7d) you are discussing.

_____

_____

_____

_____

Bibliography

American Productivity and Quality Center, *The Benchmarking Management Guide.* Portland, OR: Productivity Press, 1993.

Anderson, Bjørn, and Tom Fagerhaug, *Performance Measurement Explained, Designing and Implementing Your State-of-the-Art System.* Milwaukee, WI: ASQ Quality Press, 2002.

Anderson, Bjørn, and Pes-Gacote Peterson, *The Benchmarking Handbook: Step-by-Step Instructions.* London: Chapman and Hall, 1996.

Bacal, Robert, *Performance Management.* New York: McGraw-Hill, 1999.

Balm, Gerald J., *Benchmarking: A Practitioner's Guide for Becoming and Staying Best of Best.* Schaumburg, IL: OPMA Press, 1992. Book is based on the experiences of IBM Rochester.

Bergeson, Kathy, "Integrating and Linking Scorecards, Dashboards, and Six Sigma." IQPC Conference, October 25–27, 2004, New Orleans, LA. Retrieved March 9, 2005 from www.iqpc.co.uk/binary-data/ IQPC_CONFEVENT/pdf_file/5428.pdf

Brauerman, Joel, *Fundamentals of Statistical Quality Control.* Reston, VA: Reston Publishing, 1981.

Brown, Mark Graham, *Keeping Score.* New York: Quality Resources, 1996.

————, *Winning Score: How to Design and Implement Organizational Scorecards.* New York: Productive Press, 2000.

Burr, John T., *SPC Tools for Everyone.* Milwaukee, WI: ASQC Quality Press, 1993.

Camp, Robert C., *Benchmarking: The Search for Industry Best Practices That Lead to Superior Performance.* Milwaukee, WI: ASQC Quality Press, 1989.

————, *Business Process Benchmarking: Finding and Implementing Best Practices.* Milwaukee, WI: ASQC Quality Press, 1995.

Chang, Richard Y., and Mark Morgan, *Performance Scoreboards: Measuring the Right Things in the Real World.* San Francisco: Jossey-Bass, 2000.

Christopher, William F., and Carol G. Thor, *Handbook of Productivity Measurement and Improvement.* Cambridge, MA: Productivity Press, 1993.

Crosby, Phillip B., *Quality Is Free: The Art of Making Quality Certain.* New York: McGraw-Hill, 1979.

Felix, Glenn H., *Productivity Measurement with the Objectives Matrix.* Corvallis, OR: OPC Press, 1983. One of the basic sources for the objectives matrix.

Ford Motor Company, *Continuing Process Control and Process Capability Improvement.* Dearborn, MI: Ford Motor Company, 1987.

Galloway, Dianne, *Mapping Work Processes.* Milwaukee, WI: ASQC Quality Press, 1994.

Goldratt, Eliyahu M., *It's Not Luck.* Great Barrington, MA: The North River Press, 1994.

————, *The Goal,* 2nd ed. Great Barrington, MA: The North River Press, 1992.

Gupta, Praveen, *Six Sigma Business Scorecard: Creating a Comprehensive Corporate Performance Measurement System.* New York: McGraw-Hill, 2004.

Harry, Mikel and Schroeder, Richard, *Six Sigma—The Breakthrough Management Strategy Revolutionizing The World's Top Corporations.* New York: Doubleday, 2000.

Hayes, Bob E., *Measuring Customer Satisfaction Survey Design, Use, and Statistical Analysis Method,* 2nd ed. Milwaukee, WI: ASQ Quality Press, 1997.

Hudiburg, John J., *Winning with Quality: The FPL Story.* White Plains, NY: Quality Resources, 1991.

Imai, Mosaaki, *Kaizen.* New York: Random House, 1986.

Johnson, Perry L., *Keeping Score.* New York: Harper & Row, 1989.

Juran, J. M., *Juran's Quality Control Handbook,* 4th ed. New York: McGraw-Hill, 1988.

Counseling sessions/lectures at FPL in the 1980s by Dr. Noriaki Kano, Dr. Yoshio Kondo, Dr. Yoji Akao, and other JUSE counselors.

Kados, Will, *Operational Performance Measurement Increasing Total Productivity.* Boca Raton, FL: CRC Press, 1998.

Kaplan, Robert, and David Norton, *The Balanced Score Card: Translating Strategy into Action.* Boston: Harvard Business School Press, 1996.

Kaplan, Robert, "The Balanced Scorecard: Measures That Drive Performance" in *Harvard Business Review,* January–February 1992.

Kaydos, Wilfred J., *Operational Performance Measurement: Increasing Total Productivity.* Boca Raton, FL: St. Lucie Press, 1999.

Kula, Witold, *Measures and Men.* Princeton, NJ: Princeton University Press, 1986.

Kume, Hitoshi, *Statistical Methods for Quality Improvement.* Tokyo: The Association for Overseas Technical Scholarship, 1987.

Lily Tomlin: What Customers Want. VHS video. Norwalk, CT: Mentor Media, 1993.

Lynch, R. L., and K. C. Cross, *Measure Up: Yardstick for Continuous Improvement.* Cambridge, MA: Blackwell Business, 1991.

Maskell, R. H., *Performance Measurement for World-Class Manufacturing.* Cambridge, MA: Productivity Press, 1991.

Mears, Peter, Ph.D., *Quality Improvement Tools and Techniques.* New York: McGraw-Hill, 1995.

The Metrics Handbook, AFSC/FMC. Washington, DC: Andrews Air Force Base, 1991.

Mizurro, Shigeru, ed., *Management for Quality Improvement: The 7 New QC Tools.* Cambridge, MA: Productivity Press, 1988.

Nauman, Earl, and Kathleen Giel, *Customer Satisfaction, Measurement, and Management.* Milwaukee, WI: ASQC Quality Press, 1995.

Neely, Andy, *Business Performance Measurement.* Boston: Cambridge University Press, 2002.

Pank, Peter S., Robert P. Neuman, and Roland R. Cavanagh, *The Six Sigma Way: How GE, Motorola, and Other Top Companies Are Honing Their Performance.* New York: McGraw-Hill, 2000.

Rebholtz, David, "The World on Time." *LQRA Review.* Retrieved March 9, 2005, from www.lrqa.com/comsite/template.asp?name+comreview_fedex

Riggs, James L., and Glen H. Felix, *Productivity by Objectives.* Englewood Cliffs, NJ: Prentice-Hall, 1983. The other basic source for the objectives matrix.

Rumonler, Georg, and Alan P. Brache, *Improving Performance,* 2nd ed. San Francisco: Jossey-Bass, 1995.

More detail on the nominal group technique is found in Sink, D. Scott, *Productivity Management: Planning, Measurement and Evaluation, Control, and Improvement.* New York: Wiley, 1985.

Sink, D. Scott, and Thomas C. Tuttle, *Planning and Measurement in Your Organization of the Future.* Norcross, GA: Industrial Engineering and Management Press, 1989.

Thomas, C., "An Introduction to Operations Research and Spatial Applications at FedEx," Proceedings of AGI EORS, Thirty-Seventh Annual Symposium, September 1997.

Tsao, H-S. J., and A. Rizwan, "The Role of Intelligent Transportation Systems (ITS) in Intermodal Air Cargo Operations," Research Report UCB-ITS-RR-2000-5, Institute of Transportation Studies, University of California at Berkeley, 2000.

Wade, David, and Ron Recardo, *Corporate Performance Management: How to Build a Better Organization Through Management-Driven Strategic Alignment.* Woburn, MA: Butterworth-Heinemann, 2001.

Zelazny, Gene, *Say It with Charts: The Executive's Guide to Successful Presentations in the 1990s,* 2nd ed. Homewood, IL: Business One Irwin, 1991.

Index